Trends and Status of Minority Aging

PROCEEDINGS OF THE
EIGHTH NATIONAL INSTITUTE
ON MINORITY AGING
San Diego, California
1981

Editors:
E. Percil Stanford, Ph.D.
Shirley A. Lockery, DSW - MPA

Publisher:
University Center on Aging
College of Human Services
San Diego State University

Distributor:
The Campanile Press
San Diego State University

THE CAMPANILE PRESS
San Diego State University
San Diego, California 92182

ISBN 0-916304-57-4

*To all who not only believe
in the human value of older
minorities, but act to insure
that they fully realize their
self worth*

TABLE OF CONTENTS

Acknowledgements

In the development of any comprehensive project, a few individuals, institutions, and organizations always come to the front when critical points of work are reached. During the past years the diligence and commitment of several individuals have made the Annual Insitute on Minority Aging a success. The 1981 program is no exception. The commitment may have been greater for the 1981 program in that the task was to review issues that would certainly be prominent throughout the 80's and would be instrumental in shaping the lives of many middle-age and older minority individuals.

It is not sufficient to acknowledge only the participaiton of the many colleagues and supporters. The most important aspect of the participation that takes place in the Institute is that it is not a one-time involvement. Numerous persons have a long-term commitment to ameliorating conditions that jeorpardize a high quality of life for minority elderly. We are always tremendously grateful for the unselfish time that many participants give to the Institute. Very few persons receive remuneration for the time and effort contributed. The University Center on Aging's Planning Council is very supportive of its activities and provides suggestions for direction on a regular basis. The Council has been more than gracious in its support for the Institute on Minority Aging. A subcommittee from the Council worked with Center staff to ensure that the program would be a success. Without the sincerity of, and continuous input from, the Planning Council, we would have had a program of different quality. In addition to the Planning Council, we acknowledge the support of the College administrators and the administrators of the University. There has always been a tremendous amount of good will and encouragement from the upper level of administration.

As usual, without the hard-working staff from the University Center on Aging, it would have been impossible to sponsor the Institute from which this monograph has been developed. The staff sees the need and benefits that are derived from the Institutes which are regularly sponsored by the University Center on Aging. Many of the staff have worked more than their normal hours and have received no monetary compensation. We are sincerely appreciative of their efforts to ensure that a quality program was carried out and, further, that materials of a quality nature would be developed for enhancing the knowledge base in minority aging. Those persons who have contributed tremendously to the Institute are Maxine King, Dorothy Peckenpaugh (deceased), Ellen Reinsch, and many students who assisted on a part-time basis. In addition, many staff persons took more direct leadership responsiblity in developing the program. Those persons include Shirley A. Lockery, Kris Kyllo, and Elsie Ammann, without whom it is doubtful that we would have had a substantive program or a monograph.

It is a pleasure to be involved with individuals such as those who have contributed to this monograph. The time and effort put forth here is certainly worthy of mention. The thought and research that has gone into some of the materials has been quite time consuming. For this we owe our colleagues a great debt.

In addition to those who have submitted their presentations for publication, we would like to thank the following individuals for their contributions to the success of the Institute.

Welcome:	Albert Johnson, Vice President, SDSU, and Harriet Kopp, Acting Dean, College of Human Services, SDSU.
Community Forum Facilitators:	Alfred Elgin and Larry Curley; Delores Davis-Wong, Josephine Yelder, and Robert A. Wright; Carmela Lacayo and Daniel Gallego; Louise Kamikawa and Beverly Yip.
Keynote Presentation:	Arthur S. Flemming Leon Harper
Panelists:	Valerie L. Levy, Jessie McClure, Rudy Arrieta, Lucious McCalpine, Barry Donenfeld, Esperanze Eugenio, H. Ishikawa, Ramon Salcido, Wilford Wilson, Lupe Bickley, Charles F. Martinez, Rachel Wong, Fernando Torres-Gil, Frances Kobata, Duran Bell, Sandra Y, Nathan, & Antonio B. Rey.

I
Perspectives

E. Percil Stanford
Director
University Center on Aging
San Diego State University

OVERVIEW OF MINORITY AGING ISSUES FOR THE '80s

Overview

The Institutes on Minority Aging have continued in one form or another since 1973. The original intent of the Institute on Minority Aging was to bring persons from different ethnic and cultural backgrounds together to discuss, analyze and synthesize issues, problems and concerns still in existence, to assure the minority older person an equitable share of services and benefits. The primary purpose was to begin to look at the depth and breadth of the issues and from that point use relevant data and information to address the issues in a coherent and timely manner. The very first Institutes were small in attendence and served to provide a forum for the participants to explore the directions that might be taken to further the cause of minority older persons.

Previous Institutes on Minority Aging were successful in that they provided the one place where minority-ethnic individuals and those interested in the minority-ethnic aged could come together to discuss their concerns, uncertainties, questions and apprehensions related to matters that would have an impact on the quality of life for the ethnic older person. The Institutes have been successful in insuring that information has been disseminated to those involved in training, educational programs, planning and development and the political arena in its purest form.

In light of the 1981 White House Conference on Aging, this Institute will play a major role in insuring that relevant information, ideas and projected plans of action are widely distributed in an organized and timely fashion.

The 1981 White House Conference on Aging will pay particular attention to the concerns and interests of the minority aged, with appropriate input from the minority aged and those working with them. The input must be informed and clearly delineated. Since the 1971 White House Conference on Aging, there has been considerable effort to explicate the "true" concerns and needs of the minority elderly. Some of this work has been well planned and thought out, while much of it has yet to be formalized. It is our intention to continue to take appropriate steps to pull together individuals with the expertise and commitment to further formalize the sparse but developing information pool. By collectively and deliberately thinking through important issues, there will be an opportunity to prioritize them in a way that they can be clearly examined for possible implementation in a formal sense. One of the most important tasks is to formulate methods by which agreed-upon issues can be operationalized and made useful for the appropriate constituents.

This Institute will provide invaluable information in the content areas identified by the planning staff of the 1981 White House Conference on Aging. Our interest is to insure that the White House Conference on Aging delegates have the appropriate information and input adequately to consider the minority and ethnic issues in aging. In addition, the planning staff will have the opportunity to further use the Institute on Minority Aging to whatever advantage it sees fit. Without an Institute of this nature, it would be extremely difficult to gather comprehensive material from different ethnic groups in a manner that is cost-effective, timely and useful to the 1981 Conference.

Need for 1981 Institute on Minority Aging

There is no doubt of the continuing need for the Institute on Minority Aging. The Institutes have served to provide not only an outlet for many individuals who have taken leadership roles in the development of materials and programs, but also in ensuring the involvement of minority older persons in bringing about positive change. The Institute for 1980 set the stage for providing input into the 1981 White House Conference on Aging. The materials that have been developed to date appear to be substantial in that they are certainly designed to provide initial suggestions for the White House Conference Advisory Group and other bodies with initial input into the White House Conference itself. It is worth indicating that the mini-conferences which were sponsored by the National Minority Aging Organizations were enhanced as a result of the previous participation of these organizations at the 1980 Institute on Minority Aging. It is our hope that the materials developed at the 1980 Institute will be valuable in insuring the acknowledgement of the basic issues and ideas delineated. The four caucuses of the National Minority Organizations had an opportunity to begin to think through their strategies for further development of their positions and strategies for the White House Conference on Aging.

The need for the pre-White House Conference Institute on Minority Aging was primarily to further refine issues and begin to determine specific ways in which the identified issues could in fact be impacted. Beyond this, there is considerable strength in bringing the ethnic minority groups together to look at the similarities and differences which occur in their issue statements. Once comparisons were made, it then became reasonable to move in a direction of common strategies which could be proposed to the various levels of government. Such action began to make a difference in the resolution of some of the issues identified. On the other hand, where there were considerable differences, the full group had meaningful input in terms of clarifying positions, and also in the development of meaningful strategies to bring about solutions. In essence, it was a matter of bringing closure to the work that was started at the 1980 White House Conference Planning Sessions held by each of the minority aging organizations.

The purposes of the 1981 Institute on Minority Aging succinctly stated were to:

1. Crystallize eight years of work accomplished through the Institute for input into the 1981 White House Conference on Aging;

2. Crystallize key issues of concern to minority aging for inclusion in the agenda of the 1981 White House Conference on Aging;

3. Outline key strategies and procedures for implementing recommendations;

4. Continue to develop and organize a basic pool of minority aging knowledge;

5. Provide a forum for the exchange of the latest information among researchers, policy-makers, service providers and older people;

6. Act as a catalyst for the stimulation of future research and career preparation in the area of minority aging;

7. Facilitate long-range planning regarding minority aging issues in an effort to more decisively impact policy; and;

8. Develop strategies for disseminating information and implementing recommendations brought forth at the 1981 White House Conference on Aging.

An essential aspect of the total process was to get feedback from each minority organization that had a mini-conference. The mini-conferences best represent the latest thinking of all organizations which are oriented toward the minority aged person. The mass of data collected and synthesized by each national organization was disseminated to all Institute participants. This provided participants with the opportnity to further enhance the efforts of each of the organizations. The national organizations shared materials in a way that enriched each organization's position.

The Institute was organized to insure meaningful input from all participants. Participants were the key to the success of the Institute. Every attempt was made to keep the exchange of information open and free flowing. An atmosphere of "give and take" was established from the very beginning, and it was through this process that ideas were further clarified and delineated.

The end result of the process is to insure that there is a growing partnership between those in responsible positions with influence on minority elders and the elders themselves. During the past fifteen years, there has been more evidence that the elderly, and to a limited degree the minority elderly, have been moving toward "center stage" and taking charge of their own destiny.

It is our hope that the work of the contributors to this monograph will help provide more comprehensive directions for those minority elderly willing to take leadership.

Janet J. Levy, **Director**
California Department of Aging

NATIONAL INSTITUTE IMPACTS UPON
THE NATION'S MINORITY ELDERLY

The National Institute on Minority Aging has been a focal point for the disseminationof research findings, new developments, and practical experiences that have increased the capacity and the creativeness of people interested in maintaining the wellbeing of older minority persons. People from various states around the country have, annually during the past eight years, shared in the issues, concepts, approaches and realities of problems facing our nation's older population. We have watched the growth of the Institute over the years from what seemed to have been about 35 participants to about 200 last year. The California Department of Aging staff has benefitted from the Institute, keeping abreast of the "state of the art of aging" as it relates to the older minority person.

As a bulwark for coordination and dissemination of information, the Institute has had a positive and universal impact on planning and social policy. The role of the Institute, as we see it in the aging network, is highlighted through its leadership in developing, discussing, and this year refining, issues to be resolved at the 1981 White House Conference on Aging. Overall, delegates representing minorities and their special concerns will be some of the most adequately prepared persons ever to participate in a White House Conference on Aging. Issues that are the concern of all older persons, but that have special meaning for older minority persons, will have gone through the deliberation of participants of this Institute. Thus, some of the most knowledgeable persons in the field will have sanctioned the validity of these concerns.

From a historical perspective, we look back to the 1971 White House Conference that marked the first time that any consideration had been given to special needs of older minority persons. However, it was as late as January 29, 1971 before any substantive efforts were made to include the special concerns of older minority persons. In contrast, for the 1981 conference over 20 months of planning will have gone into identifying and refining issues. Significantly, older minority persons themselves will have had the opportunity to develop the issues. For the 1971 conference there had been no actively organized vehicle, such as this Institute, to pursue real issues that jeopardized the wellbeing of older minority persons. Fortunately, under the leadership of the late Hobart C. Jackson of Philadelphia, and others noted authorites in aging (Inabel B. Lindsay,

D.S.W.; Jacquelyne J. Jackson, Ph.D.; M. Powell Lawton, Ph.D.; Elias S. Cohen, MPA, J.D.; Robert Kastenbaum, Ph.D.) and the support of the National Council on Aging and the American Association of Homes for the Aging, an organized effort was activated. Attention to the 1971 Conference's inadequate planning came late. As Jerome Waldie, previous Executive Director of the 1981 Conference, stated, ". . . the one day set aside for special concerns of minorities was a euphemism for minority consciences of particular areas of concern."

We are becoming a society with an increasing number of older persons. Although longevity is not the same for all ethnic groups, the percentage of older persons in each ethnic group ccontinues to increase. An increased older population, a decrease in the nation's birth rate, coupled with the fact that this country is in a decreasing state of productivity, will necessitate a redirection of scarce resources. Aging programs and older people will feel the "brunt" of the cuts in federal, state and local budgets. Perhaps not as quickly in the next few years, but certainly the rippling effects of unemployment, inflation, tight money in areas of education, health and social welfare will impact the lives of all older Americans.

In the report prepared for the 1981 White House Conference by the Subcommittee on Human Services, Select Committee on Aging, the subcommittee refers to the ". . . growing numbers and proportions of seniors as a triumph—one for which this country can be justly proud." I concur with the subcommittee. I am convinced, however, that we must adequately identify and resolve the problems that face us now, for the way we deal with the problems and concerns of our aging population today will certainly determine the wellbeing of all of us (the now-greying society) of tomorrow. This poses a tremendous challenge to all of us in developing, refinging and presenting issues to the state and White House conferences on aging of 1981.

Contrary to the traditional belief that younger people are abandoning older persons; that families, neighborhoods and religious groups are neglecting the older persons; research after research points out the deep involvement of family members, etc. (our natural supports) with the older person. As a society, we must focus on our natural supports as the key to the wellbeing of the older person in the future. There must be a sharing of services—older persons teaching/ younger persons learning; both receiving and giving, building and maintaining social and cultural values. One may refer to this as an intergenerational approach to the psycho-social wellbeing of the American people.

In California, the legislature has funded a model program to determine the social and economic benefits derived from providing the older person an opportunity to reduce his or her food cost by receiving a nutritious meal in exchange for the use of his or her skills, expertise and cultural experience to broaden the cultural experiences of the children. The program is called the Senior Nutrition and Volunteer Services Program. It provides an intergenerational approach to volunteerism. Findings from the evaluation of the program indicate that the psychological wellbeing of the older person participating in this program is far more significant to the individual than the monetary benefits from receiving a meal. The meal may satisfy a need for a short period of time; however, the satisfaction derived from feeling needed, accepted and valued increases the self-esteem of both the older and the younger person and make both their days worth living. The most unique experiences from this program have come from the older Hispanic persons involved in it. Where many programs have found it difficult to involve older Hispanic persons in volunteer services, these programs (one in San Diego and one in Sacramento) have shown that acceptable surroundings and appropriate supervision by people who are able to relate to the Hispanic culture can bring about immeasurable results.

The future direction of aging should focus on intergenerational services. Available resources should be used to assist in the development of the natural support system—the family, the neighborhood, the religious groups and voluntary association—an integration of several generations. Scarce resources should be directed toward receiving maximum benefits with increased quality and accessibility to the older person. Making our natural support systems an effective part of our delivery system will also mean the need to recognize and legitimize the differences among racial and ethnic subgroups—especially in the senior population. The creative use of the service potential in natural community-based minority groups is essential in order to have a significant impact on the wellbeing of older persons whose cultural differences must be valued to make their lives meaningful.

"The 1971 White House Conference on Aging sought to crystallize in National Policy the dimensions of a society in which older Americans may 'fitly' live while completing the adventure of life with fulfillment and serentiy." The Conference moved toward a National Policy on Aging. This conference, the 1981 Conference on Aging, is geared to making a National Policy on Aging a reality. You are taking an active role in shaping that policy. Millions of older persons will stand to benefit from your work at this Institute.

I will close with an age-old parable: It seems that there was a very wise old gentleman who lived in the hills of a small rural area. The people of the village valued his wisdom and sought him out regularly for his wise sayings and direction. The younger people were amazed at his intellect, so much so that one young man became very jealous of the attention being given to the old man. He told his friend that he had decided to "stump" the old man with a question. His plan was to catch a bird, clutch it in his palms and ask the old gentleman whether the bird was living or dead. If he says, "it is dead," I'll open my hands and let the bird fly away. If he says, "it is alive," I'll destroy it with the pressure of my hands. They found the old gentleman and posed the question. The wise old gentleman looked at the young man with a sympathetic smile and said, "It's in your hands, you make the decisions."

II

Minority Aging:
Current Status and
Future Directions

José B. Cuellar, Ph.D.
Associate Director for Research
University Center on Aging
San Diego State University

INTRODUCTION

A decade ago when the seminal essays on minority aging precursors Donald Kent, Richard Kalish, Sam Yuen, Joan Moore, Jacqueline Jackson and others were published in the special issue of *The Gerontologist*, there were fewer than 80 research publications on the subject. Today we estimate that there are close to 1,500 written research reports and discussions that deal with minority aging experiences. Since 1971 there has been a significant increase in the number of gerontologists who have contributed to the development of this new area of specialization.

During the past decade, the combined efforts of a great number of persons have resulted in the establishment of the National Center/Caucus on Aging, the Asociación Nacional Pro Personas Mayores, the National Indian Council on Aging, the Pacific/Asian Resource Center on Aging, and the National Hispanic Council on Aging. Within the past five years, these organizations have significantly impacted the development of minority aging activities by influencing the way public resources have been allocated.

Although there have been a number of critical reviews of literature on minority aging research during the past decade, until now there has been no attempt to systematically collect, organize, and assess the state of the art. The timely significance of the current effort is underscored by the recent recommendations to Congress of the Select Committee on Aging presented in a report: *Future Direction in Aging Policy: A Human Service Model*. It is particularly important now to review what we know and what we need to know regarding the conditions and needs of minority older persons in face of the major changes for the next set of Older Americans Act Amendments proposed in the report:

1. that the full floor of services be mandated only for those age 75 plus and those who are functionally dependent before this age;

2. that the Administration on Aging's dispersement authority be removed to the Department of the Treasury, which will handle fiscal matters through a Special Office of Adult Affairs;

3.   that all present Title XX services to the elderly be merged under the Older Americans Act;

4.   that Area Agencies on Aging support and utilize fully in-place systems—families, neighborhoods, voluntary and religious associations, and racial/ethnic subgroups;

5.   that the emphasis of care systems be on prevention, early detections and self-help healing;

6.   that tacit support be given to: (a) elimination of all mandatory retirement; (b) rigid enforcement of age discrimination laws; (c) reduced tax rates for older workers, and tax exempt retirement income; (d) tax credits for those who care for elders; and (e) inclusion of specific home health component for elders in national health insurance policies.

The fact that this report by the Select Committee on Aging, published in May 1980, completely ignores the research findings on the effects of minority status on the conditions and circumstances of a significant proportion of older persons who need services the most must be underscored. It gives no consideration convincing to all of that data that argue that minority elders exist with multiple needs, indeed in multiple jeopardy—with older females in greatest need. It also fails to recognize fully the extreme importance of the ethnic factor in the process of successful service delivery.

Last year, in collaboration with four of the minority aging organizations, the University Center on Aging, San Diego State University, with a grant from the Administration on Aging, initiated the process of codifying available research on minority aging. Over the past year the project has scanned volumes of literature, and acquired and indexed more than 750 works, or little more than half of the total literature identified. A preliminary analysis has led to the following tentative conclusions regarding the state of the art:

1.   The subject areas that have received the most attention are physical and mental health, housing, employment and income. Those that have received the least attention are nutrition, transportation, leisure and recreation. The subject of family relationships has not been totally ignored, but neither has it received the attention it deserves.

2.   One of five works in minority aging remains unpublished, therefore very difficult to acquire. Another fifth of the literature can be found in conference proceedings or as chapters in books. With the remainder found in professional journals (mostly *The Gerontologist*).

3.   Almost three-fifths of the literature focuses on older persons in one specific group or another, with the noticeable increase in multi-

ethnic or cross-cultural comparative research during the past five years. Aging in the black experience has received the most attention, and has been the subject of almost half of the available minority aging literature. Hispanic older persons, United States Mexicans in particular, have been the subject of the next largest number of reports; followed by Pacific/Asians. American Indian older persons, in general, have received the least amount of research attention. Next to nothing is known about the specifics of aging in the Alaskan, Hawaiian, Puerto Rican Island, United States and Cuban experiences.

In order to assess the state of the art with respect to service delivery, four nationally prominent gerontologists were commissioned, on recommendation of the respective minority aging organizations, to address the most important issues involved in human services to older persons in each of the major minority groups, identify gaps in knowledge and trends for the future, by focusing on the series of options that comprise the proposed Human Service Model:

1. Who should receive priority for senior services?

2. Should the service system be multi-ethnic or ethnic-specific/age-integrated or age-specific?

3. Should the orientation be prevention or treatment?

4. Should the emphasis be on acute or long-term care?

5. Should the scope be limited or comprehensive?

6. Should policy making and service provision be centralized or decentralized?

7. And, how should public and private resources necessary to adequately address the needs of the most vulnerable elders be incorporated?

As should be obvious by now, the uneven quantity and quality of research available on various topics and ethnic minorities have magnified significantly the difficulty of the task undertaken by the presenters that follow, which makes us appreciate their work that much more.

John Red Horse, Ph.D.
Associate Professor
School of Social Work
Arizona State University
Tempe, Arizona

AMERICAN INDIAN AND ALASKAN NATIVE ELDERS: A POLICY CRITIQUE

This chapter examines public policy in aging with particular attention to the impact it may have upon American Indians and Alaskan Natives. Discussion is guided by the framework offered in the "Future Directions in Aging Policy: A Human Service Model." The initial material contains an overview of the functions of policy with reference to the ordering of institutional priorities based upon social forecasting. This is followed by specific treatment of the model as organized into three units: (1) age related factors, (2) service strategies, and (3) organizational strategies. Each unit is examined in light of related literature and concerns of key informants. The conclusions pose selceted implications for research, education, and training.

Functions of Public Policy:
Public policy fosters a course of action through principles which guide institutional behavior. It organizes according to national priorities, thereby influencing appropriations, regulations, and interventions. Public policy may be divided into two broad, though not mutually exclusive, types: reactive and proactive. Reactive policy is ameliorative. It evolves after problems are observed and guides corrective or compensatory interventions through institutional responses that provide social or economic supports, such as Aid to Families with Dependent Children. Reactive policy seldom attempts to solve chronic social problems; rather, it insures the "truly needy" entitled level of support for daily living.

Proactive policy is quite different in character and intent. This type of policy, following Gil (1970), anticipates relationships among individuals as aggregate units, forcasts future roles, statuses and needs among the population, and launches resource distribution plans accordingly. Proactive policy, therefore, initiates national priorities and influences future quality of life in the United States. In other words, it is designed ostensibly to avert chronic social problems. It encourages primary prevention and highly effective secondary intervention.

The Model, much to its credit, clearly represents proactive policy. Prediction through social forecasting, however, raises serious questions regarding appropriateness of the Model for American Indian and Alaskan Native populations. The Model is predicated upon trends derived from analyses of demographic, biomedical and gerontological data. Clearly, errors of omission prevail. Through analyses of census data the Model anticipates a society that is proportionally growing older and establishes an old-old cohort, i.e., 75+, as the fastest growing segment in society. Literature specific to American Indian and Alaskan Native populations, however, points to an opposite trend: they are represented by a generally young population. Median age for American Indian and Alaskan Natives is estimated at approximately 17 years while that for whites ranges from 28 to 30 years (Benedict, 1971; Hill and Spector, 1971). Moreover, life expectancy rates among American Indian and Alaskan Native elderly are significantly lower than for the white population (Human Resources Corporation, 1978). Life expectancy rates among American Indians and Alaskan Natives have increased dramatically in recent years? however, this can hardly be construed as a trend. Life expectancy rates tend to fluctuate from year to year among all population groups. A variety of medical and socio-environmental circumstances make this fluctuation more dramatic among American Indians and Alaskan Natives (Bell, Kasschau, and Zellman, 1976).

The age trend factor is exacerbated by death phenomena. American Indians and Alaskan Natives have significantly higher probability of dying before age 65 than do whites. There is some correlation across the population groups in that heart disease, stroke, and cancer are leading causes of death. Proportionally, however, diseases of the heart, stroke, and cancer account for only 53 percent of deaths among American Indian and Alaskan Native groups compared to 75 percent among whites (Benedict, 1971). Other causative factors of a compelling nature emerge. For numerous years accidents represented the leading cause of death among American Indians and Alaskan Natives. This should not prove surprising given their hazardous social circumstances common to rural poverty (Bell, Kasschau, Zellman, 1976). Chronic illnesses, whether poverty-related or not, contribute disproportionately to mortality rates among American Indians and Alaskan Natives as compared to whites: cirrhosis of the liver, five times higher; influenza and pneumonia, two and a half times higher; diabetes mellitus, two and a half times higher; tuberculosis, eight times higher. Any institutional planning for preventive health care for American Indian and Alaskan Native elders must obviously account for these population specific morbidity factors (Human Resources Corporation, 1978).

Ascertaining trends among American Indian and Alaskan Native populations through census or other government counts is a tentative process at best. Estimates of proportions of elders among these groups vary from less than 5 percent (Benedict, 1971) to 11.6 percent (Manson, 1980). The reasons for the variations range from definitions of Indian and Alaskan Native status to effectiveness of data collection procedures. The Bureau of Census methodology in 1970, for example, included Indians living only within 115 reservation areas. Indians on trust lands outside reservation areas were categorically excluded. Moreover, a tracking of the Social Security Administration's benefit statistics for 1975 revealed that the racial classification, American Indian, was omitted (Human Resources Corporation, 1978).

The aforementioned issues are not raised to criticize the concept of model building in public policy, but rather to articulate that social forecasting is dependent upon input data for projection. Omission of representative data reflecting life circumstances among American Indian and Alaskan Native populations suggests that planners and decision makers have proceeded with policy formulation in a one-dimensional manner. The obvious note here is that new data inputs are necessary. The Model represents a mainstream statement which without specific protective provisions, such as fiscal set-asides for culture and population specific programs, will undoubtedly place American Indians and Alaskan Natives at a disadvantage and quite possibly outside the protection of social regulations. With this general thought in mind, let us turn attention to the particulars of the Model.

Age Related Factors

Age-related factors of the Model address two critical questions: who should receive senior services, and should a future service system for seniors be age-integrated or age-specific? Areas of mental, physical, social, economic and daily task capabilities are identified as units by which functional independence can be evaluated. Chronological age *per se* is discarded as a predictor of need except at 75 years of age. "Natural seasons of life" are presented as more logical in today's society whereby senior adults (60-75) are presumed to be functionally independent persons and elder adults (75+) are presumed to be functionally dependent persons. Individuals in the senior adulthood cohort would qualify for services but these would be age-integrated with adult services in general and would entail elaborate screening procedures. Elders (75+) would be served separately. Moreover, because the elderhood cohort is identified as the fastest-growing segment of the American population, it rightly serves as the priority target group: the 75+ cohort has first rights and represents the focus of the future aging policy.

These propositions advanced by the Model pose alarming threats to the wellbeing of American Indian and Alaskan Native elders. Presumptions around the target group (75+) are especially onerous. The aging process varies among population groups according to life circumstances. Recent research has drawn attention to significant differences in the aging process between American Indians and Alaskan Natives as a group and non-Indian populations. The National Indian Council on Aging (NICOA) (1981) compared life conditions among American Indian and Alaskan Native elders with a baseline non-Indian population from Cleveland, Ohio. Two major research findings around character of life and the aging process were:

1. The character of life for Indians and Alaskan Natives aged 45 and older is significantly different than that of the dominant population.

2. Impairment levels of Indians and Alaskan Natives 55 and older are comparable to Cleveland elderly 65 and older. Rural Indians and Alaskan Natives 45 and older are comparable to Cleveland elderly 65 and older. (p. 31)

These findings suggest a need for cultural adjustments around the "seasons of life." The critical period for prevention and early identification among

American Indian and Alaskan Native populations appears to be 45 to 65 years of age. Excluding these years from priority focus in future aging policy places elders within these populations into "quadruple jeopardy": they are poor, old, minority and members of subpopulations with a wrong age distribution vis-a-vis the general population. American Indian and Alaskan Native elders become old before the proper time: far too many never arrive at the "season of life" to qualify as a priority. First Americans will seldom benefit from "first rights."

The character of life finding by the National Indian Council on Aging deserves further comment. Table 1 identifies selected concerns raised by American Indian and Alaskan Native key informants regarding services provided for elders in these respective populations. These represent time and again repeated, ubiquitous and compelling cultural issues emanating from tribal people with distinctive characters of life. These cultural factors transcend physical and emotional deprivations that American Indians and Alaskan Natives entering the critical years of life, I.e., 45-65 years of age, have endured through chronic disease, chronic unemployment, and chronic sub-nutrituion. Character of life introduces a complexity of tribes, a strength of families, and a dramatic resistance to health and social services controlled by non-Indians. Each of these impact the activities implied in the Model which are required to make distinctions around the "seasons of life," i.e., evaluation of functional independence, needs assessment and the setting of eligibility criteria and launching of intake systems.

Table 1.

Age, Assessment and Evaluation Factors Identified
by American Indian and Alaskan Native Key Informants *

Historical Experience
Inconsistency of Service Networks in Adapting to Cultural Differences
Culturally Insensitive Intake Systems and Procedures
Need to Honor and Work with Spiritual Beliefs
Need to Lower Age Eligibility Requirements
Culture Shock in Nursing Home Services
Clan and Kinship Behavior
Cultural Weighting of Eligibility Criteria
Define Eligibility According to Tribal Standards
Provide for Unmet Nutritional Needs
Need for Interpreters
Staff Programs with Indian Administrators and Line Workers

*All key informant tables were derived from formal resolutions passed by the General Assembly at the National Indian Council on Aging Conference, Albuquerque, New Mexico, Fall, 1980.

The complexity of tribes introduces issues of legal status and differences in cultures, languages, and historical experiences. There are 293 federally recognized tribes and 58 without such legal status. According to life style factors, these tribes may be organized into 9 to 17 separate cultural areas with 149 distinct languages generally spoken on a daily basis by elders (Manson, 1980). Language appears as a significant issue in the delivery of health and social services. Thirty-six percent of American Indian elders speak native languages (American Indian Nurses Association, 1978). One source suggests that less than 3 percent of reservation elders are proficient in the English language (Native American Consultants, Inc., 1978). Dukepoo (1980) surveyed elders in Southern California and noted that 49 percent of the reservation sample experienced difficulty with English language forms. Finally, the social history of tribes guides a strong sense of belonging and community aspiration. A strong identification with tribe and custom represents an unresolved issue with the aging service network. Lustig (1977) indicated much dissatisfaction in nursing homes among Indians who were uprooted from their tribal communities and randomly placed with elders of other tribes.

Community and tribal preferences are reflected through a tightknittedness and strong bonding in American Indian families. Red Horse and his associates (1976) identify a particular set of strengths organized around traditional structural patterns of extended family and kinship systems. These strengths impact both social and health behaviors. The National Indian Council on Aging (1981) provides further insights into the intensity, frequency, and types of daily interactions characteristic of elders within family systems as well as the close proximity of family members. Family structure clearly influences "level of perceived need, awareness of available service, and actual use of said services" (Manson, 1980, p. 20). Kniep-Hardy and Burkhardt (1977) suggest that extended family and traditional religion must be integral to intake and diagnostic procedures and to the delivery of medical services designed for Navajo patients.

The Model, of course, does not include substantive assurances that cultural and tribal specific asjustments to facilitate early identification, rapid assessment, and treatment will assume priority status.

Service Strategies

Service strategies of the Model address several critical questions: what kind of services should be offered, should a preventive or treatment orientation be employed, should acute or long-term care be emphasized, and should services be limited or comprehensive? Primary prevention, i.e., promotion and maintenance of independence, and secondary prevention, i.e., early detection and treatment, represent mainstays of the Model. Prevention is cited as a long-overdue strategy to bolster a well-planned lifelong and comprehesive service continuum. A comprehensive service continuum represents a commitment to revise care as service needs change through the course of life. Thus, acute and long term care will be tailored to benefit the target group of elders (75+). Services to younger groups are based on assumptions of limited needs, emphasizing assessment, referral, and advocacy. The pillars of comprehensive care, i.e., outreach, evaluation, and case management, would be reserved as unconditional activities for the 75+ population group. Community services and institutional care are included in the comprehensive service package.

These propositions of the Model presume that an effective institutional arrangement of health care and social services is in place. All that remains is strategic refinement thorugh with senior adults (60-75) would receive full floor comprehensive services. In the case of American Indian and Alaskan Native populations, the obvious and critical question is ignored: how will referral and advocacy effectively serve elders who are not now reaping benefits of minimum care and have probably never enjoy full services for which they qualify? This becomes of particular concern since the Model proposes to remove these elders from the "presumed need" list and place another barrier between them and mainstream quality of care by virtue of age criteria.

Equality of opportunity is a common argument advanced by American institutions. Agency personnel glibly suggest that health and social service institutions are designed to serve the entire population. Efforts to date have been less than satisfactory. In basic public assistance service, for example, underutilization commensurate to need by American Indians appears common in all regions of the United States (Bell, Kasschau, and Zellman, 1976). American Indians demonstrate more reluctance to use community mental health centers than other populations, and in cases where visits are made show a significantly higher dropout rate than other patient groups (Sue, 1977).

Table 2 identifies related concerns raised by American Indian and Alaskan Native key informants regarding problems in service delivery to elders. These issues include network behavior, elder involvement in programs, and comprehensive care strategies. These concerns also represent a modest and polite effort to articulate minimum cultural features necessary for a comprehensive strategy in aging policy. Modern institutional norms do not coincide with traditional Indian views concerning health and mutual aid. This has fostered "*dis*-ease" and underutilization. Dukepoo (1980) identified fear and mistrust among Indian clients as fueled by insensitive agency personnel as major barriers to service delivery. Little and Shoop (1976) suggest that one strategy to relieve the "*dis*-ease" of fear and distress in institutional care of elders would be to provide Indian staff for service delivery. This strategy appears supported in a community survey among Minneapolis urban Indians who overwhelming indicated preferences to be served by Indian personnel (De Geyndt, 1973). Needless to say, American Indians "*dis*-ease" fosters a level of health well below American standards in general.

Elder American Indian concumers have witnessed viable alternatives designed to fit cultural customs. Nevada, for example, has modified institutional and home health care program that varies with the seasons: Spring services are home-centered, consisting of in-home visits for administration of medication, cleanings, and othr assistance; Winter services are residential, with elders placed in local institutional care facilities (Indian Nurses Association, 1978). This plan allows maximum physical protection during time periods when transportation of health personnel is hindered and minimizes psychological distress because elders realize that they will return home soon.

The Nevada program bears testimony that the sense of family roles among elders remains strong. Research on perceived and actual status (Manson and

Table 2.

Service Strategy Issues in Prevention, Type of Care, and Comprehensiveness
Identified by American Indian and Alaskan Key Informants*

Need Culture-Based Institutional Care
Religious Freedom
Develop Re-entry Strategies Back to Family
Develop Nursing Homes on the Reservation
Observe Network Behavior within Tribes, Villages and Indian Organizations
Support Indigenous Networks to Prevent Premature Institutionalization
Create Elderly Board of Investigators to Accredit Institutional Care
Support Elder-to-Elder Services
Train Elders in Program Planning, Monitoring and Evalution
Develop More Parallel Services
Adapt to Tribal Remoteness
Eliminate Population Requirements of Title VI
Eliminate Barriers to Coordination
Develop Age-Integrated Cultural and Educational Centers
Develop Model Projects Designed to Track Effective Service to Elders
Expand Community Health Representative Force
Expand Training for Indian Professionals

*All key informant tables were derived from formal resolutions passed by the General
Assembly at the National Indian Council on Aging Conference, Albuquerque, New Mexico,
Fall, 1980.

Pambrun, 1979) and perceived filial responsibility (Barber, Cook, and Ackerman,
1980) are mixed and inconclusive. Nevertheless, the sense of family responsibility
appears to be a lifestyle feature that remains crucial in health care plans. Red
Horse (1980) identifies this sense of family as a particular aspect of ego integrity
characteristic of life span development in American Indian extended family
systems. Curley (1978) captures this as a process of role transition for a Navajo
elder. This need of continuing family roles was corroborated by The National
Indian Council on Aging (1981). It appears sufficient to say that regardless of
functional dependence or independence, family re-entry appears as a critical
feature of any comprehensive care strategy for American Indian and Alaskan
Native elders.

    The sense of family introduces awesome challenges for the Model. Exist-
ing health and social services offered to American Indian and Alaskan Native
elders have not been supportive of indigenous family philosophies. There are
some compelling reasons for this lack of responsiveness. Tribal size, natural
resources, and remoteness of reservations serve as barometers of fiscal capacity
and opportunity to develop viable strategies. Elders from isolated reservations

are especially vulnerable to removal from family and community against their choice. Moreover, existing regulations guiding services to elders incorporate service barriers to remote reservations. Population requirements, for example, appear as a particular point of stress. Unless requirements are relaxed, equal opportunity will remain an empty promise simple because of variations in the elderly populations among tribes. This ranges from 5.6 percent (Levy, 1967) to 13 percent (Williams, 1980) of tribal population. While these differential statuses of tribes are overlooked in the Model they are in the forefront among concerns of American Indian and Alaskan Native key informants.

Organizational Strategies

Organizational strategies of the Model address two basic questions: should services be centralized or decentralized and will resources derive from the public or private sector? Decentralization through local authority is emphasized. Local Area Agencies on Aging will coordinate assessment, referral and advocacy for senior adults (60-75) and full-floor services for the elders (75+) with all previously defined responsibilities of outreach, evaluation and case management. Local Area Agencies on Aging would become a complete aging resource for training and service coordination. Fiscal distribution would be through direct grants to states following the two-tiered service system, i.e., funds for senior adults (60-75) would channel through the general system of adult services, and funds for the elders (75+) would channgel though the Older Americans Act with subsequent distribution following state plans. The Administration on Aging would assume a role as national resource to consult on policy and technical assistance needs. The Model advocates a dismantling of institutional superstructure and a re-empowerment of inplace service groups closest to the aging constituency, i.e., community-based mediating structures identified as family, neighborhood groups, voluntary associations, religious groups, and ethnic groups.

Following earlier discussion, the conceptual scheme of decentralization and re-empowerment advanced by the Model are in many respects compatible with the needs and aspirations of American Indian and Alaskan Native elders. Problems identified with the leviathan of public institutions are mirrored in concerns among the Indian communities. Table 3 identifies selected issues raised by American Indian and Alaskan Native key informants regarding program and organizational strategies. Issues of coordination, compliance and transfer of technology to tribes are prominent in the listing. Collectively these capture a ubiquitous sense of rising expectations. Tribes routinely have been assured tribal sovereignty and self-determination through policy statements. These derive from the unique historical relationship emanating from treaties between tribes and the federal government. Tribes recognize that this relationship has been contaminated by public programs that route resources and regulations through states and result in a maze of bureaucratic barriers to service delivery, much to the agony of American Indian and Alaskan Native elders.

Coordination to improve the quality of care emerges as a problem in three major service networks: (1) Federal programs designed to serve the aging population in general, (2) state programs designed to serve the aging population in general, and (3) programs mandated to serve Indian populations only. American Indian and Alaskan Native elders are, of course, entitled to any service provided through federal Acts, whether this be direct or inderect. An array of programs lacking coordination results. While many programs have mandates around coordination, this in no way assures that such will occur. Indeed, mandates requiring coordination on one federal law or often contradicted by contrary mandates in related federal laws. In this sense, legal institutional barriers actually hinder coordination of programs to elders (NICOA, 1981). Lack of coordination is evident also at state levels. A survey of mental health programs in Oregon uncovered considerable overlap of responsibilities among agencies, with a noted absence of coordination in actual delivery of services (Manson, 1980). Coordination issues also impact intake systems. This is patently evident in programs mandated to serve only American Indian populations. An array of eligibility criteria emerged as a result of differential definitions of Indian status (NICOA, 1981; Bell, Kasschau, and Zellman, 1976).

Table 3.

Program and Organizational Strategy Issues Identified by American Indian and Alaskan Native Key Informants*

Establish Indian Aging Desks in The Administration on Aging, Bureau of Indian Affairs, and Indian Health Service

Establish an Indian Ombudsman in Health Care

Eliminate Barriers to Coordination

Develop a Single Set of Eligibility Criteria to Coordinate Federal Programs

Establish the National Indian Council on Aging as National, Contractor, Monitor, and Coordinator

Increase Funds for Transportation, Titled Programs, and Training

Allocate 100 Percent Nutrition Funds from Title VI

Revise Food Program Eligibility

Comply with Earlier Findings in Needs Assessment

Recognize Special Legal Relationship Between Tribes and Federal Government

Existing Federal Programs Often not Consistent with Federal Tribal Relationships

Responsibility of Tribes in Social Services Ignored by Administration on Aging

Redefine Eligibility Standards to Fit Tribal Definitions of Need and Needy

Need Compliance for Aging Services by the Bureau of Indian Affairs and Indian Health Service

Revise Fiscal Channels to Establish Direct Funding of Tribes

*All key informant tables were derived from formal resolutions passed by the General Assembly at the National Indian Council on Aging Conference, Albuquerqye, New Mexico, Fall, 1980.

Compliance reflects the lack of follow-through and response to stated needs among American Indian and Alaskan Native elders. Their relative deprivation is not a new discovery, but a nagging and long-term concern. An early work suggested that Indian elders are" . . . the most deprived identifiable group of American citizens" (Benedict, 1971, p. 51). The 1971 White House Conference on Aging compiled 29 specific recommendations regarding Indian elderly. These identified needs around extreme deprivation in income, housing, nutrition, transportation, and health. The major themes guiding these early recommendations mirror the aggregate concerns of the American Indian and Alaskan Native key informants employed by the current work. Nevertheless, investigators have found no evidence that the 1971 recommendations have been acted upon (Human Resources Corporation, 1978; Manson and Pambrun, 1979).

American Indian and Alaskan Native elders and tribal organizations are quite patient, but both groups recognize that coordination and compliance issues appear insoluble because key actors around those issues are beyond grassroots control. Thus elders and tribes alike endorse decentralization, but differ from the Model in a major respect: they call for a transfer of technology through direct funding of tribal organizations by the federal government. This is not as dramatic as it sounds since Title VI of the Older Americans Act provides for direct funding (NICOA, 1981). Direct funding, moreover, appears in accord with tribal sovereignty and self-determination and would bypass state Area Agencies on Aging. American Indian and Alaskan Native priorities would not be subordinated to other state agenda.

Direct funding to tribes is not simply an issue of money, but an issue of capacity building. Several state units on aging, for example, allocate per capita funds for Indian elders in excess of their proportional population. An analysis of the priorities around the use of such funds, however, indicates differences between state and tribal strategies: states are prone to feed funds back into in-place public institutions while tribal organizations set a priority on capacity building through training of indigenous personnel (NICOA, 1981). Thus, following the Model, tribes see direct funding as a mechanism to facilitate "natural systems" of family, neighborhoods, and ethnic groups.

Summary Discussion

This paper has examined issues pertinent to the future "Directions in Aging Policy: A Human Service Model." The discussion has focussed upon the concerns and life circumstances of American Indian and Alaskan Native elders. While the Model sets forth important and compelling principles, several of its assumptions were challenged. Primary among these were assumptions regarding the aging process, population trends, and availablity of services through existing institutional networks. Presumptions such as these could precipitate institutional barriers to service in the absence of appropriate tools to culturally match assessment, evaluation and case management of the needs of American Indian and Alaskan Native elders.

The discussion has by no means been exhaustive. The integration of available literature with identified concerns of American Indian and Alaskan Native key informants, highlights several areas that impact research, education, and training. Among these are: (1) the need for an adequate data base that captures a representative picture of elders and of the numerous tribes and Alaskan Native villages; (2) the need for cultural inquiry of the aging process so that primary prevention strategies can be organized according to life situations and chronic diseases confronting American Indian and Alaskan Native elders; and, (3) the need to develop and appraise culturally matched services through the launching of community-based demonstration services.

Finally, a massive program of training and technical assistance should be developed to facilitate a transfer of technology. A direct funding strategy provides a logical avenue through which the Model can adapt to tribal and village complexity and honor federal commitments to tribal sovereignty and self-determination. Given the startling differences of needs and priorities between tribal groups and the general population specific earmarked funds appear necessary to assure that first Americans will benefit from "first rights."

References

American Indian Nurses Association. Alternatives for planning a continuum of care for elderly American Indians. In *The continuum of life: Health concerns of the Indian elderly*. Albuquerque, New Mexico: National Indian Council on Aging, 1979.

Barker, C.E., Cook, A., & Ackerman, A. *Attitudes of Navajo youth toward supporting aged parents.* Paper presented at the 33rd Annual Meeting of the Gerontological Society of American Indians, San Diego, California, November 1980.

Bell, D., Kasschau, P., & Zellman, G. *Delivery services to elderly members of minority groups: A critical review of the literature.* Santa Monica, California: The Rand Corporation, 1976.

Benedict, R. A profile of Indian aged. In *Minority aged in America* (Occasional Papers in Gerontology, No. 10), Institute of Gerontology: University of Michigan and Wayne State Univesity, 1971.

Curley, L. Retirement: An Indian perspective. In E. P. Stanford, (Ed.), *Retirement: concepts and realities.* San Diego, California: The Campanile Press, San Diego State University, 1978.

DeGeyndt, W. Health behavior and health needs of urban Indians in Minneapolis. *Health Service Reports*, 1973, *88*, 360-366.

Dukepoo, C. *The elder american Indian.* San Diego, California: The Campanile Press, San Diego State University, 1980.

Gil, D.E. A systematic approach to social policy analysis. *Social Service Review*, 1970, *44*, 411-426.

Hill, C.A., Jr., & Spector, M. Natality and mortality of the American Indian compared with U. S. whites and non-whites. *HSMHA Health Report*, 1971, *86*, 229-246.

Human Services Corporation. American Indian Elderly. *Policy issues concerning the minority elderly: Final report*. March, 1978: 1-56.

Kniep-Hardy, M., & Burkhardt, M. A. Nursing the Navajo. *American Journal of Nursing*, 1977, 77, 95-96.

Levy, J.E. The older American Indian. In E. G. Youmans, (Ed.), *Older rural Americans: A sociological perspective*. Lexington: University of Kentucky Press, 1967.

Little, P.F., & Shoop, M.R. Extended care services for the elderly Indian: A study of the Gila River Indian community. In J. Lyon, (Ed.), *The Indian elder: A forgotten American*. Washington, D.C.: National Tribal Chairmen's Associaton, 1978.

Lustig, J. *The needs of elderly Indians in Phoenix, Arizona: Recommendations for services*. Phoenix, Arizona: Affiliation of Arizona Indian Center, Inc., 1978.

Manson, S.M. *Cultural determinants of mental health programming and service delivery to American Indian and Alaskan Native elderly*. Paper presented at a special session on minority elderly convened at Lake Tahoe, California. Sacramenta: California State University, Institute for Human Service Management, July 1980.

Manson, S.M., & Pambrun, A.M. Social and psychological status of the American Indian elderly: past research, current advocacy, and future inquiry. *White Cloud Journal*, 1979, 1, 18-25.

National Indian Council on Aging. *Program research for serving the Indian elderly*. Forthcoming, 1971. Albuquerque, New Mexico.

Native American Consultants, Inc. *Research project methodology for national survey of older Indians and needs assessment*. Washington, D.C.: Native American Consultants, Inc., 1978.

Red Horse, J.G. American Indian elders: unifers of Indian families. *Social Casework*, 1980, 61, 490-493.

Red Horse, J.G., Lewis, R., Feit, M., & Decker, J. Family behavior of urban American Indians. *Social Casework*, 1978, 59, 67-72.

Sue, S. Community mental health services to minority groups: some optimism, some pessimism. *American Psychologist*, 1977, 32, 616-624.

Williams, G.C. Warriors no more: A study of the American Indian elderly. In C. L. Fry (Ed.), *Aging in culture and society*. New York: Praeger Publishers, 1980.

Maurice Jackson, Ph.D.
Department of Sociology
University of California at Riverside

THE BLACK AGED AND THE HUMAN SERVICE MODEL

This chapter attempts to apply the Human Service Model to knowledge of the black aged. The Model facilitates the bringing together of issues in the serving of the needs of elderly persons and relevant data. It addresses seven basic issues: 1) priority of service receivers—should persons up to or persons over the age of 75 receive services first? 2) relation to other age groups—should the service be age-integrated or age-specific? 3) orientation of services—should it stress a preventive or treatment approach? 4) basic approach of services—should it emphasize acute or long-term care? 5) scope of services—should it be limited or comprehensive? 6) base of services—should it be centralized or decentralized? 7) source of resources for services—should it be based on public or private sources?

The Select Committee on Aging's response to these choices is that persons over 75 years of age have first rights to service, and that the service must be preventive, decentralized and based upon resources from the private sector. For these elders, services should be comprehensive, long-term, age-specific. In contrast, for seniors below 75 years of age, the services should be limited, acute, and age-integrated.

The Human Service Model is predicated upon several assumptions: 1) the public sector which has been responsible for most of the services to seniors is greatly overextended; 2) fiscal resources are decreasing; 3) hence, there is not enough money available today nor will there be enough in the future to meet the needs of tody's seniors; 4) seniors over 75 years of age are the fastest-growing segment in our population; 5) they are also most in need and therefore should have priority on services.

This analysis will relate data on the black aged to the Model in order to determine how a future human service model for the black aged will look. In contrast to the Model, it assumes that the situation and circumstances of the black aged must be examined as a distinct group in each component of the Model rather than just treated as part of a natural support system of the private sector, and that redistribution of resources to the aged is not a new requirement brought about by demographic changes but one necessitated by the cultural value of equality.

Before relating knowledge of the black aged to the Human Service Model, I want to say something about that knowledge, published and unpublished, which has accumulated since 1975, the starting point of our analysis. First, the studies of this last decade represent the first decade of intensive and extensive study of the black aged in the history of the country.

Comparing a study on the black aged published a decade ago with the list of references collected by the University Center on Aging at San Diego State University demonstrates much greater interest in the black aged in the last five years (Jackson, 1971).

The earlier bibliographic study reported 71 items (58 percent which were published) over a period of 20 years, from 1950 to 1971. On the list of bibliographic references from 1975 supplied by the University Center on Aging, there were 60 items on black aged (77 percent of which were published) and 77 (70 percent of which were published) on minority elderly: The combination of references on black and minority elderly yields 137 works (73 percent of which were published). In this six-year period more than twice the number of relevant articles were written than were produced in the earlier 20-year period.

The earlier study concluded that very little was known about elderly blacks since they were not the object of systematic study. Furthermore, the research focused on social status rather than the aging process. To some extent today, a data base on the black aged is being compiled, although there still exist many deficiencies and gaps in our research knowledge.

For this first draft of an evaluation of the Human Service Model in terms of the black aged, we have examined some articles, but this report will have to be regarded as provisional and subject to change as we continue our examination of other works, Also, for this draft, rather than to assess the quality of knowledge on an article-to-article basis, I accepted their individual conclusions. In effect, we will base our judgment here on informed opinion as well as scientific data.

The first question of the Human Service Model regarding who has the first right to service is the most important one. The Model specifies 75 years of age as the cutting point between independent (those younger than 75) and dependent (those older than 75) seniors. This decision merely compounds the problem of using chronological age as the criterion for determining eligibility for delivery of service (Stanford, 1980). Black have lower life expectancy (Bell, et. al., 1967; Daly, 1976; Greene, 1977; Jackson, 1979; Williams, 1980) and if services were first given to those over 75, far fewer blacks would benefit from the existing services.

The Model does suggest that a functional age criterion be employed in addition to the chronological one. This takes into account the fact that some persons are older at an earlier age than others and that chronological age is not the best measure of aging. In short, the black aged have been punished by use of an age-criterion of eligiblity that is not based upon their life situations. Employment of even an older age of eligiblity will not increase the punishment.

This point notwithstanding, knowledge of the black aged leads to the conclusion that they should either be the highest priority for service or, at least, be considered as much a prime target as persons over 75. The Human Service Model declares that the aged over 75 are poorer, sicker, less educated, and more likely to be dependent on family, friends, community support, and the government. This can virtually be said for the black aged. In contrast to the white aged, they are poorer (Cantor, 1976; Daly, 1976; U.S. Bureau of Census, 1978; Williams, 1980), sicker (Cain, 1980; Prim, 1977; Williams, 1980), less educated (Bell, et.al., 1976; U.S. Bureau of Census, 1978) and more likely to be dependent on the family (Cantor, 1976; Jackson and Wood, 1976; Williams, 1980). In addition, their housing is poorer (Johnson, 1978), and their life expectancy is lower (Bell et.al., 1976; Daly, 1976; Greene, 1977; Jackson, 1979; Williams, 1980). If services should be granted first to those most in need, the black aged would rank first since their needs are so much greater.

Not only are the black elderly more needy than white elderly, but their population is increasing at a faster rate than both the general population and the white elderly. This means that unless great efforts are undertaken now, there will be a larger population of persons with severe needs, which cannot be met by services aimed first at the aged over 75.

Although it is quite clear that the need for service is very great for the black aged, it may be very difficult if not impossible to give them first priority for services. At the very least, we suggest that any service model that becomes law give great attention to the black aged so that their situation will not become exacerbated. In lieu of priority service, it is apparent that the black aged need affirmative action to relieve their circumstances. Without such efforts the equality in care that is a hallmark of a democracy will not be achieved.

With regard to relationship to other groups, the Human Service Model suggests that service to those over 75 be age-specific and those under 75 age-integrated. This matter has not been one of serious research into the black elderly's situation. One study (Cantor, 1979) does conclude that aged black women who were integrated with the younger generation were better off than women living alone. It would appear, on the one hand, that to the extent it is true that the black aged are in close contact with the other age groups, age-integrated services would be appropriate. On the other hand, it might be argued that the problems of the black aged are so severe that only age-specific services will begin to ameliorate them. One other matter needs to be considered here and in the other components of the Human Service Model. It is the existence of change, its direction and speed. Hurling (1978) claims that the number of black aged living with their offspring is on the decline; therefore, it would appear that age-specific services will become more appropriate.

cute needs to that which emphasized long-term needs. Services for acute care can be included. The multiple, long-enduring problems of the black aged seem number of investigators (Cain, 1980; Cantor, 1976; Eve, 1979; Faulkner et.al., 1975; Guttman, 1980; Laurie, 1980; Rao, 1980; Scott and Kivett, 1980; Wright, 1979), there is yet no firm agreement as to which approach is more suitable for the black aged. Guttman, (1980) reports that the high degree of unawareness of services by the black aged makes prevention difficult if not impossible. Conversely, increase in awareness of service would lead to a greater possibility of preventive services. Cantor (1976) claims that little money for adequate care makes treatment, let alone prevention, difficult to achieve. A low degree of understanding of services by the black aged led Laurie (1980) to claim that prevention is difficult for them to achieve. On the other hand, Wright (1979) argues that prevention is possible to the extent outreach and follow-up clinics are developed, while Cain (1980) claims that the more critical health problems of aged blacks require preventive service.

In general, prevention is a useful ideal; it can reduce the need for treatment. However, treatment may be more appropriate for populations in trouble. Once the problems are treated it will be easier to institute preventive services. Perhaps some populations need both services. Finally, a change from treatment to preventive services may require changes in health seeking practices.

The Human Service Model proposes a change from care in reaction to acute needs to that which emphasized long-term needs. Services for acute care can be included. The multiple, long-enduring problems of the black aged seem to require long-term services. More severe impairment at lower ages (Laurie, 1980); less availability of home care (Engler, 1980; chronic conditions (Williams, 1980); less access to nursing homes (Jackson, 1978); lower education (Tallmer, 1977) and similar problems of the black aged make long-term services necessary. The extent to which these difficulties stem from racism (Dancy, 1977; Henry, 1977) discrimination Engler, 1980) and cultural barriers to services (Kivett and Learner, 1980) makes long-term care imperative.

According to the Human Service Model the scope of services should be limited for seniors under 75 and comprehensive for elders over 75. The former need only assessment, referral and advocacy; the latter, outreach, evaluation and case management. For aged blacks the opinion seems to be that their wide range of needs requires comprehensive services. Barriers to health care (housing, income etc.) are seen as needing comprehensive care and attention (Bell et.al., 1976; Gordon, 1979), as do poor and chronic health problems (Williams, 1980); low awareness of existing services (Gordon, 1979; Prim, 1977); triple jeopardy (Daly, 1976); and cultural barriers to services (Kivett and Learner, 1980).

The next component of the Human Services Model addresses the issue of centralization versus decentralization. A decentralized approach is suggested in which the federal government provides money directly to the states. In turn the local Area Agencies on Aging primarily responsible for elders over 75 would also be responsible for assessment, referral, and advocacy for those seniors under 75.

This is an oversimplified version of the Human Service Model's resolution of the issue of centralization-decentralization; but it is sufficient for our purposes.

The last component involves the use of public or private source of resources for services to the elderly. The Human Service Model would utilize private sources. Since these last two components parallel each other, I will respond to both together before discussing them separately. In assessing the success or failure of the federal government and the public sector in serving the elderly, it is not enough to emphasize the role of the states and the private sector as a meaningful alternative. Both the state governments and the private sector have been less involved than the federal government and the public sector in giving services to the black elderly. In fact, the development of services by the federal government has been more than appropriate—otherwise, the situation of the elderly, including those persons over 75 years of age, would be best termed a disaster. A more useful approach might be to use the strength of both federal and state governments and of both public and private sectors. At the least, any criticism of the role of the federal government and public sector needs to be complemented by a critical assessment of the roles of the states and private sectors in serving the elderly.

The last component of the Human Service Model stresses the need for empowering private natural support systems such as the family, neighborhoods, voluntary associations, religious groups, and ethnic groups. I have already commented on the inadequacy of the model's treatment of blacks as a support group, which is the only instance in which minority groups are discussed.

Much more research needs to be conducted on these natural systems. The evidence on the supportive aspects of the family of the black aged are contradictory. Dancy (1977) argued that older blacks rely greatly on the supportive services of their families. Hurling (n. d.) found intergenerational conflict in a black community. Seebach (1980) reported no difference between black and white aged in the filial responsibility of their adult offsprings toward them. Bell and his associates (1976) summed this up as a set of contradictions in the strengths of families for the black aged. Clearly, more research is needed in this area.

One study (Clemente, 1975) found voluntary associations to be more important to the black aged than the white aged. Older blacks belonged to more associations and had higher attendance rates. Clemente attributes this to the higher proportion of church associations to which older black belonged. Religion has been viewed as very important among the black aged (Dancy, 1977). Jackson and Wood (1976) also found religion to be considered more important by the black aged.

To facilitate evaluation of the private/public segment of the Human Service Model, it is necessary to research the influence of neighborhoods and racial identity on the black aged. It will also be useful to examine the services older blacks perform for other groups in their communities and in the nation.

This summary briefly treats the major points that were made relative to the various components of the human service model. First, the problem with emphasizing priority of the 75 years and over age group compounds the problem for the black aged as their life expectancy is short; therefore, fewer blacks would benefit from this priority. Functional age criteria would be more suitable to the black aged. Black aged should rank among the top with respect to need for services, and affirmative action is strongly needed for the black aged.

Second, to the extent it is true that black aged are in close contact with other age groups it would appear that age-integrated services would be more appropriate. However, target age specific services may reduce the plight of the black aged more since the services would be expressly directed at them. Also, due to the apparent decrease of blacks living with offspring, it would be more appropriate to focus on age-specific services.

Third, both treatment and preventive services would better serve the black aged. The high degree of unawareness of services by the black aged makes prevention impossible, although prevention is the ideal approach. No firm agreement has been established on this issue. This indicates a great need for future research in this area.

Fourth, long-term care is imperative to the black aged. The multiple, long-enduring problems of the black aged require long-term services.

Fifth, comprehensive services are needed for aged blacks. Barriers to health care, housing, income and so on show a need for comprehensive care.

Sixth, a centralized approach or some combination of the strengths of both the federal government and the state governments appears to be more suitable to the life situation of the black aged.

Seventh, it is difficult at this time to determine the extent to which private natural systems are more supportive for the black aged than the white aged and the degree to which the public or private sector renders more service. The magnitude of the situation of older blacks in the future may well call for a more intensive effort on the part of both public and private sectors.

The Human Service Model proposed that persons over 75 years of age be granted the first rights to service which must be preventive, decentralized and based upon private resources. Service can be limited or comprehensive, acute or long-term, or age-integrated or specific depending upon whether persons are older or younger than 75.

The Human Service Model applied to the black aged makes no age distinction. Service needs to be long-term and comprehensive and either age-integrated or specific, preventive or treatment oriented, centralized or decentralized, and public or private or some combination.

These models, to the extent to which these distinctions are valid, differ enough that it will be necessary to make a special effort to meet the needs of the black aged if the Human Service Model becomes law.

References

Bell, D., et. al., Characteristics of the black elderly. Rand Corporation. Reprinted with permission from *Delivering services to elderly members of minority groups: A critical review of the literature*, R 1862-HEW, pp. 81-103, 1976.

Cain, L. *Sociocultural factors which affect the need for and the use of mental health services by the minority elderly.* Paper presented Conf. on Services for Minority Eldery, Inst. Human Serv. Mngt. CA. 7-80.

Cantor, M.H., Rosenthal, K., & Wilker, L. Social and family relationships of black aged women in New York City. *Journal of Minority Aging*, 1979, 50-61.

Cantor, M., & Mayer, M. Health and the inner city elderly. *The Gerontologist*, 1976, *16 (1)I*, 17-25.

Clements, F., Rexroad, P.A., Hirsch, C. The participation of the black aged in voluntary associations. *Journal of Gerontology*, 1975, *30 (4)*, 469-472.

Daly, F.Y. To be black, poor, female and old. Reprinted from *Freedomways Magazine*, 1976, *16 (4)*.

Dancy, J., Jr., *The black elderly: A guide for practitioners.* The Institute of Gerontology. The University of Michigan-Wayne State University, 1977.

Engler, M. *The impact of ethnicity on home care needs: A comparison of black and white elderly*. Prepared for presentation at 33rd Annual Scientific Meeting of Gerontological Society, San Diego, California, November 21-25, 1980.

Eve, S.B., & Friedsam, H.J. Ethnic differences in the use of health care services among older Texans. *Journal of Minority Aging*, 1979, *4*, 62-75.

Faulkner, A.O., Heisel, M.A., Simms, P. Life strengths and life stresses: Explorations in the measurement of the mental health of the black aged. *American Journal of Orthopsychiatry*, 1975, *45 (1)*, 102-110.

Gordon, J.U. Use of aging services by elderly blacks in Douglas County, Kansas. *Journal of Minority Aging*, 1979, *4*, 88-92.

Greene, D. Health indicators and life expectancy of the black aged: Policy implications. In W. Watson, et. al. *Health and the black aged*. Washington, D.C.: The National Center on the Black Aged, 1977.

Guttmann, D. *Strategies for increased utilization of public benefits by minority elderly*. Presented at Conference on Provision of Services to Minority Elderly, July 23, 1980, Lake Tahoe, California.

Henry, M. Perceived health status of the black elderly in an urban area: Findings of a survey research project. In W. Watson, et.al., *Health and the black aged*. *Proceedings of a research symposium: May 27, 1977*. Washington, D.C.: The National Center on Black Aged, 1977.

Huling, W.E. Evolving family roles for the black elderly. *Aging*, September/October 1978, pp. 21-27.

Huling, W.E. *Conflict between generations in a blck suburban community*. Center for Education and Research in Gerontology, Counseling Center, California State University, Northridge.

Jackson, J.J. Negro Aged: Toward needed research in social gerontology. *The Gerontologist*, Part II, 1971: 52-57.

Jackson, J.J. Special health problems of aged blacks. *Aging*, September/October 1978, pp. 15-20.

Jackson, J.J. Epidemiological aspects of mental illness among aged black women and men. *Journal of Minority Aging*, 1979, 76-87.

Jackson, J.J. Aging black families and federal policies: Some critical issues. *Journal of Minority Aging*, 1979, *5 (1)*, 162-169.

Jackson, M., & Wood, J.L. *Aging in America: Implications for the black Aged*. Washington, D.C.: The National Council on the Aging, Inc., 1976.

Johnson, R. Barriers to adequate housing for elderly blacks. *Aging*, 1978, pp. 33-39.

Kivett, V.R., & Learner, R.M., *The rural elderly poor: Economic Impacts and policy Issues*. Presented at 33rd Annual Scientific Meeting of Gerontological Society, San Diego, California, November 1980.

Laurie, W.F. *Use of services: A difference exists*. Federal Council on the Aging, Washington, D.C., 1980.

Primm, B.J. Poverty, folk remedies and drug misuse among the black elderly. In Watson, W., et. al, *Health and the black aged, proceedings of a research symposium.* Washington, D.C.: The National Center on Black Aged, 1977.

Rao, V.N., & Rao, V.V.P. *An evaluation of the life satisfaction index among the black elderly.* Presented at Annual Meeting of the Gerontological Society of America, San Diego, California, November, 1980.

Scott, J.P., & Kivett, V.R. The widowed, black, older adult in the rural south: Implications for policy. *Family Relations,* 1980, 83-90.

Seelbach, W.D. *Filial responsibility among aged parents: A racial comparison.* Presented at 33rd Annual Meeting of Gerontological Society, San Diego, California, November 1980.

Stanford, E.P. *Functional age as criteria for determining eligiblity for services.* Paper presented at meeting of Institute for Human Service Management, Lake Tahoe, California, July 23, 1980.

Talmer, M. Some factors in the education of older members of minority groups. *Journal of Geriatric Psychiatry,* 1977, *10 (1),* 89-98.

United States Bureau of the Census. *Social and economic characteristics of the older population: 1978.* (Special Studies Series P-23, No. 85). Washington, D.C., 1978.

Williams, B.S. *Characteristics of the black elderly.* (1980, 5), U.S. Department of Health and Human Services, 1980.

Wright, R., et. al., Medical care and the elder: An exploratory analysis of factors involved in the use of physicians' services by black and white elderly. *Journal of Minority Aging,* 1979, 5 *(1),* 123-129.

Wright, R., et. al., The black elderly and their use of health care services: A causal analysis. *Journal of Gerontological Work,* 1979, 2 *(1),* 11-27.

Jean Keith Crawford, Ph.D.
Lecturer
Department of Sociology
California State University at Fullerton

ANALYSIS OF THE "HUMAN SERVICE MODEL" IN TERMS OF OLDER HISPANICS

The Human Service Model is an attempt by the Subcommittee on Human Services to readjust and reapportion dwindling federal funds for aging programs. Unfortunately for minorities, the Model is formulated to accommodate the mean, or average, older person in the society. When evaluated as a useful instrument for older Hispanics, the Model falls short of minimal expectations when judged in terms of either needs for or equity in the system. If the option positions assumed by the Subcommittee become translated into policy, it will mean once again, that those in greatest need will receive the least assistance.

The current problem facing policy makers constitutes the horns of a dilemma. Not only are funds for the aged becoming more scarce, but the population of aged is steadily increasing. In short, there are fewer dollars to be spread among more individuals just when money buys less.

The fast-changing shape and size of the population pyramid comes as no big surprise. We have been forewarned by demographers who are reasonably accurate in projecting population specifics—based on past and present trends. It will be around 2015 before the peak of the 1940's baby boom turns 65. According to Uhlenberg (1977) a stationary population may not be reached until about 2050. Until that time, we can expect ever-increasing proportions of aged in the population. While social scientists and policy makers were prepared to take into account increasing numbers of aged in the population, few were prepared for the cut backs in funds which have become a present reality.

The Human Service Model is composed of seven options, each of which deals with a specific service provision. Taken together, the options answer questions regarding what, for whom, and how services will be provided. The Subcommittee has adopted a platform position on each option. The purpose of this address is to: 1) Evaluate the Subcommittee's position on each option in terms of appropriateness and equity for older Hispanics; 2) Draw on the literature, when available, to shed light on the specific situation of older Hispanics, and; 3) Comment on factors which must be considered before equity can be approached for older Hispanics.

Option One

The option considers the question: Who should receive priority for senior services? The Subcommittee proposes that allocation be based on the criterion of age, with individuals 75 years of age and older receiving first priority to services. The priority of this age group is based on the logic that those over 75 constitute the aged group of highest need. However, in practice an important condition which should be noted is that this is the age group which will grow most rapidly in the future. Given limited resources, it therefore, stands to reason that we could envision future expenditures only for those 75 years of age or older, should this option be translated into policy.

The question of present concern is how the imposition of an age criterion of 75 and over would affect older Hispanics. In order to answer this, we must ask yet another question—namely, what are the chief differences between Hispanic elderly and elderly in the dominant population? Some of the important differences are:

1) As a group, older Hispanics are more likely to be economically disadvantaged. Mean income is lower, and older Hispanics are twice as apt to live below the poverty line as are Anglos (Persons of Spanish Origin in the United States, Bureau of the Census, 1977).

2) Life expectancy is shorter for older Hispanics than for Anglos (Moustafa and Weiss, 1968).

3) Older Hispanics are members of a minority group and as such are subject to multiple disadvantages that accompany minority status.

These are only three of the variables on which older Hispanics are more disadvantaged. The cumulative effect has important implications for their lives. In addition, researchers must consider the interactional effect of minority status, shorter life expectancy, and lower income. Getting back to the central question—How would the imposition of an age criterion of 75 and over affect older Hispanics?—we can now state: Older Hispanics would be adversely affected by the policy were it to become reality. Lower socioeconomic status among older Hispanics leads to shorter life expectancy, which means a lower probability of ever reaching age 75. Therefore, limiting services to those aged 75 and over eliminates with one stroke a whole group of older individuals from the competition for the available funds. This is a clear case of inequity in the distribution of resources, and can be seen as further discrimination against a group who already suffer multiple disadvantages.

Option Two

The option is concerned with the question: Should a future service system for seniors be age-integrated or age-specific? The Subcommittee had adopted the posture that the 60-75 year age group should not be served separately, but that the 75-year-old and older group should be served separately. This option shares with Option One the group which is identified for service priorities, but the logic on which the conclusion is based is somewhat different.

The logic for the position taken on Option Two rests on the premises of developmental theory.

The basic argument of nearly every developmental paradigm is that for in the way they think of themselves or their environment (Hendricks and Hendricks, 1977). Developmental psychologists have therefore assumed that individuals face similar tasks in adjusting to different stages as they pass through life. Following this same line of thought, the Subcommittee proposed that at about age 75 individuals become more dependent on outside help. This conclusion is backed by research findings, but it fails to take into consideration one main provision of developmental paradigms—that of making allowances and adjustments for unusual group characteristics.

The position assumed by the Subcommittee fails to take into consideration the particular life circumstances of older Hispanics. Most would be inadvertently excluded by the adoption of this model due to their low representation in the 75-and-over age group. Option Two, as it now stands, would work decidedly to the detriment of all older Hispanics.

Option Three

The issue is: What kind of services should be involved? Should the model employ a preventive or treatment orientation? The Subcommittee has opted to endorse the preventive approach. The preventive emphasis works best when the population at risk has had access to adequate social services in the past. The plan works less well when the population needs acute care—especially medical care. Preventive care is meaningless when acute care is warranted. For this reason, a preventive emphasis, without treatment, would not fulfill the needs of older Hispanics. The proportion of use to need is very low among older Hispanics. The Needs Assessment Study (Crawford, 1980) indicated that among Mexican Americans, 73.6 percent reported a need for services which are not currently being received. So long as older Hispanics share unequally in the resources of this country, a model which includes both treatment and prevention must be used to insure minimal services to the "most needy of the needy".

Option Four

The question addressed is: In our approach to human services, should we emphasize acute or long-term care? The Subcommittee had adopted the stand that the emphasis should be on long-term care. In general terms, the weight of the evidence is on the side of long-term care—though we are in unknown waters in terms of research to evaluate the model. This is because the prevailing mode of care in this country has been "acute care". Where nursing home utilization has been studied, it has been noted that Hispanics tend to be minimally represented. Eribes (1977) noted that Mexican Americans were dramatically underrepresented in the resident population of nursing homes in Arizona. Also, Eribes noted that as income goes up, the probability of nursing home institutionalization goes down—suggesting that such care is reserved as a last resort.

On the other hand, there is evidence that living patterns are changing among Hispanics in our post industrial society. Ragan and Bengtson (1977), reported from a community survey that Mexican Americans prefer to live with their children, but the younger generation does not want to take care of the aged as before. Cuellar and Weeks (1980) reported that 50 percent of older Hispanics in their sample lived alone. Other findings suggest that older Hispanics who live alone use more social services than those who live in other arrangements (Crawford, 1980). If these findings correctly reflect changes underway in our society, we can expect older Hispanics to utilize nursing homes to a greater extent. At this point, there have been no studies to determine why older Hispanics use nursing homes less than their porportion in the general society would suggest is appropriate. Therefore, more research is needed to assess whether personal or demographic factors, or a combination of the two, comprise the opposition currently exhibited by older HIspanics. The long-term-care model represents the forward look for the future, but it must be tempered with acute care where needed.

Option Five

What is the scope of services that should be available? Should they be limited or comprehensive? The Subcommittee agrees that services to senior adults (60-75) should be limited, while services to elders (75 and over) should be comprehensive. For older Hispanics, this approach is unsatisfactory for the same reasons that the positions accumed on Option One and Option Two were unsatisfactory. The objection is based on the disjunction between perceived age (which seems to be related to health) and chronological age, wherein older Mexican Americans see themselves as older than their chronological age justifies. For older Hispanics, the position taken by the Subcommittee is unsatisfactory because services are to be limited to those who are between 60 and 75 years of age. Among older Hispanics, age 60 is old—while age 75 may never be attained.

Option Six

The question of centralization or decentralization is especially important for minorities, because when decentralization is the model, minorities are usually shortchanged. The hazards of turning over funds and their discretionary use to local authorities are many. One important one is that, in the absence of a central government, the funds can be disbursed according to arbitrary criteria. Such practices usually work to the disadvantage to minority groups. Block grants on a per-capita basis is not the way to insure equitable social services where minorities are numbered among the population.

Option Seven

The question posed is: Will the many resources needed for our Human Service System be found in the public or in the private sector? The Subcommittee chooses to emphasize the private sector across the board. The "mediating structures" include the family, neighborhoods, voluntary associations, religious groups, and ethnic groups.

Among older Hispanics, the main source of help has always been the private sector, so that is nothing new. Crawford (1980) reported that fewer than 5 percent of older Hispanics receive sustained financial support on a regular basis from informal networks. Valle and Mendoza (1978) found that 1.8 percent of the older Latinos included in the San Diego study were dependent upon family for assistance. Therefore, it helps very little to reinvest the primary group as "caretakers" when the financial support they give is practically nil. I assume that the intent of the position taken by the Subcommittee is that family and community should never have been left out when considering the care of the aged. They do and should supply emotional support and financial support when possible. On the other hand, to expect disadvantaged groups to provide care for the aged when the resources at their disposal are very limited is to expect the impossible. Ways should be explored to insure that the older person maintains in the community. Some of the innovative approaches which have already been suggested include incentives and other kinds of rewards to primary group caretakers.

Older Hispanics have never shared equally with other older individuals in the American Dream. Though many have lived for many years in their present neighborhoods, and though they have worked hard during that time, they are less likely to receive Social Security benefits at age 65 than are their Anglo counterparts. In the Needs Assessment Study, 51 percent of older Mexican Americans had resided for 20 years or more in their present neighborhood (Crawford, 1980). On the basis of this information, older Mexican Americans can hardly be considered a transient population. Even so, only 55 percent participate in Social Security benefits. This compares with 76 percent of Anglos of the same age (office of the Los Angeles Mayor, 1975). For Mexican Americans, years of work may not eventuate in Social Security benefits.

It is presumptous for one researcher to propose a model that will equitably serve the older population in this country. In a democracy as diverse as ours input must necessarily be by many, especially ethnic advocates and researchers. Even so, it seems appropriate to suggest at this time that any model which proports to include equitable services to older Hispanics take into consideration their high contributions to this country, previous exclusion from the system, their unique life conditions, and their present and past high need for services. Any equitable solution to the distribution of social services must take these considerations into account. As Cuellar and Weeks (1980) have so aptly concluded, equity in the delivery of services to minority elders resides in the utilization of "need" as criterion for eligibility.

References

Crawford, J.K. *A national study to assess the service needs of the Hispanic elderly.* Los Angeles: Asociación Nacional Pro Personas Mayores, 1980.

Cuellar, José B., & Weeks, J. *Minority elderly Americans: A prototype for area agencies on aging.* San Diego: Allied Home Health Association, 1980.

Eribes. R.A., & Bradley-Rawls, M. *The underutilization of nursing homes facilities by Mexican American elderly in the Southwest.* (Unpublished paper presented at the Annual Meeting of the Gerontological Society, 1977).

Hendricks, J., & Hendricks, C.D. *Aging in mass society: Myths and realities.* Cambridge, Massachusetts: Winthrop Publishers, Inc., 1977.

Moustafa, A. T., & Weiss, G. *Mexican-American study project: Health status and practices of Mexican Americans.* Los Angeles: School of Public Health, University of California, Division of Medical and Hospital Administration, 1968.

Ragan, P., & Bengston, V. *Aging among blacks, Mexican Americans, and whites: Development, procedures, and results of the community survey.* (Unpublished paper from the Community Survey), Andrus Center, University of Southern California, Los Angeles, California, 1977.

Uhlenberg, P. Changing structure of the older population of the USA during the twentieth centruy. *The Gerontologist,* 1977, *17 (3),* 197-202.

United States Department of Commerce. *Persons of Spanish Origin in the U.S.: March 1976.* Current Populating Reports, Series P-20, No. 310, Washington, D.C.: U.S. Government Printing Office, 1977.

Valle, R., & Mendoza, L. *The elder Latino.* San Diego, California: The Campanile Press, San Diego State University, 1978.

Sharon Y. Moriwaki, Ph.D.
Program Administrator
State of Hawaii
Department of Labor and Industrial Relations

UPDATE OF CURRENT STATUS OF
AND FUTURE DIRECTIONS FOR
ETHNIC MINORITY ELDERLY GROUPS: PACIFIC/ASIANS

As we look with anticipation toward the upcoming White House Conference on Aging, (WHCOA) we should look toward building on the achievements of the past ten years. It was at the last WHCOA—not quite ten years ago—that the Asian/Pacific Islanders discovered that they were excluded from the special concerns sessions for minority groups. Regardless of the reasons cited for this oversight, the Asian Americans did succeed in having their Special Concerns Session. What is important is that 1971 marks the year in which the Asian/Pacific elderly became visible—in which it was recognized that they had problems and needs in many respects even more intense and complex than those of the general elderly population. Since then, progress has been made primarily in research and advocacy efforts—such as the Pacific/Asian Elderly Research Project (P/AERP); the inclusion of Chinese, Guamanian, filipino, and Japanese groups in the San Diego State University cross-cultural study; as well as the more recently funded National Pacific/Asian Resource Center on Aging (P/ARCA). Service programs for Pacific/Asian populations have also emerged, e.g. the Chinatown and Koreisha nutrition projects in Los Angeles; the Union of Pan Asian Communities (UPAC) "home helps" in San Diego, and the On Lok Center in San Francisco.

The 1970's then, saw the expansion of services to the elderly. However, the decade of the 80's does not portend as well for minority elders who have just begun to receive some of the benefits of the social services system. The new administration, in its proposed massive cuts in human services in the name of "economic recovery," makes the Nixon Administration's "benign neglect" policy look meek. The consequence of social services being on the "hit list" is a "divide and conquer" policy, with all sectors fighting each other for the biggest piece of a shrinking pie rather than working together for a bigger pie. I hope that all of us here and your representatives to the National White House Conference on Aging will not be coopted into this stratagem, but will work together for the best interests of all our elderly.

The current status of minority aging, although improved during the past decade, is still highly fragmented and inconclusive. Perhaps the San Diego University Center on Aging "minority codification project" will correct this. Although it will assist us, codification is possible only if we have data to codify. The project to date has compiled the literature on minority aging—some 348 listings. Of these, approximately 38 deal with Pacific/Asians; but only 16 (less than 5 percent) are based on empirical data. Most of these are profiles based on census data and needs assessments of individual ethnic communities or descriptions of services to various Pacific/Asian groups. A comprehensive and representative national data base other than the 1970 Census data—which by the way have not accurately profiled our elderly population—is grossly lacking. Improvements are forthcoming in the 1980 Census, but those data will not be available until the fall of this year or the spring of next year.

As I understand it, our task during this Institute is to develop recommendations for the WHCOA as well as for the Older Americans Act which will be reviewed by Congress this year. We have been asked to focus on the options for a future aging policy as proposed by the Congressional Subcommittee on Human Services. With this as a framework, let me proceed to some background on the Congressional Subcommittee's proposal. In light of the national mood for decreased government spending and efforts to provide better services at no additional cost, the Congressional Subcommittee on Human Services proposed its policy on aging in terms of seven options for a "human service model". These options were predicated on giving first rights to those who are presumed to be most functionally dependent, i.e., elders 75 years and older. Based on this premise, it proceeded to place priority on age-specific, long-term care and comprehensive services to those age 75 and older. Those under 75 are to be limited to assessment, referral, and advocacy services since they are to use the existing age-integrated adult services system. Within this context—and somewhat contrarily—emphasis is on prevention rather than treatment. Finally, to implement this "human service model," the subcommittee proposed that program and policy decisionmaking be decentralized, and that private sector agencies and natural support groups be the primary deliverers of services.

In light of this proposal, I reviewed once again the studies on Pacific/Asian elderly. Unfortunately, although we do have research on Pacific/Asian elders, these data were not adequate to address the issues proposed by the Subcommittee. The most critical option proposed is that of defining the target group for services—this undergirds all other options. The major question for those of us concerned about the wellbeing of Pacific/Asian elders: What will be the impact of an aging policy based on providing comprehensive services only to those 75 years and older?

To answer this question adequately we would need accurate age-specific data on the needs of each of our Pacific/Asian groups. These are, in terms of population size from largest to smallest: Japanese, Chinese, Filipino, Hawaiian, Korean, Guamanian, Samoan, other Pacific Islanders, and the newer immigrants of Southeast Asian ancestry. We would need to assess their health and economic status, supports, and use of multiple services and benefits. The little research and data we do have only partially address this issue. Before citing these data, or the lack thereof, in their relation to potential impact of the seven proposed options, several basic attributes of Pacific Asian elderly must be acknowledged:

1.   As an ethnic minority group, the Pacific/Asian elderly, aged 65 and older, number a little over 100,000. Although this comprises

one-half of 1 percent of the total U.S. population in this age category, the growth rate of the Chinese, Japanese and Filipino elders was three to five times higher than their white counterparts during the period between 1960 and 1970.

It is expected therefore that the 1980 Census, in addition to avoiding the undercounting of the 1970 Census, will show a large proportion of Pacific/Asian elderly to the total population. Another factor supporting this expectation is the increasing influx of immigrants from Pacific and Asia. For example, the increase between 1965 and 1973 for Koreans was 959 percent and for Filipinos, 883 percent.

2.   As a minority group, the Pacific/Asian includes the disparate Oceanic cultures of Micronesia and Polynesia as well as the culturally distinct groups from Asia. In addition, as with all other minority groups, the diverse subgroups within each major ethnic groups defy simplification of any sort. Immigration patterns, socio-economic status, generational differences, and a host of other elements contribute to the heterogeneity of this minority group.

Another factor which must be acknowledged particularly in reference to the Pacific Islanders is the need to differentiate between those who have migrated to the mainland U.S. and to Hawaii, and those that reside in U.S. jurisdictions. Although confronted with rapid changes associated with advancing technology and "Americanization," these jurisdictions perceive their needs as different from those who have emigrated.

3.   The Pacific/Asian population is clearly clustered in certain geographic regions. 1975 estimated indicate that one-third reside in California; one-fourth in Hawaii, Other concentrations occur in the larger cities. The 1970 census indicated that 90 percent of Asian-American elderly lived in urban areas, compared to the national average of 73 percent. Although largely urban, there are nonetheless strong regional differences. The services for Hawaii's Pacific/Asian elderly, for example, are ethnic-integrated while those on the West Coast are ethnic-specific. For the Pacific jurisdictions, the delivery modalities will also be necessarily different from those elsewhere.

4.   The majority of Chinese, Japanese and Filipino are foreign born, with the highest proportion—82 percent—among the Filipinos. Additionally, among the Chinese and Japanese elderly, 80 percent are not fluent in English.

5.   In terms of health levels, the study by José Cuellar on equity in benefits to minority elders in San Diego may shed some light. Included in his sample were Filipinos, Samoans, Guamanians,

Japanese, Chinese and Korean elders. Although age-specific analyses have not been conducted, data are available for further analyses by age. What the data indicate, however, is that all these Pacific/ Asian groups, except for the Filipino and Japanese, rated their health as poor or very poor more frequently than did their non-minority counterparts. Further, the severity of needs was greater than non-minority elders in a number different areas other than health; such as income, housing, transportation, and, more importantly, information on services and benefits available to them.

As found here and in other studies such as the San Diego Cross-Cultural Study, the Catholic University study of equity in benefits for minorities in Washington, D.C. and the P/AERP survey of service providers, Pacific/Asians form a highly heterogenous category, and do have needs, which unfortunately are not served by the formal service system—a point to which I will return to later.

Now, to the options of the Subcommittee. To answer more cogently the issue of providing comprehensive services only to those elders 75 years and older, we need only look at the age distribution of chronic diseases where the individual is incapacitated and in need of multiple services. These data are not available by ethnic group and by age breakdowns; however, some data were obtained for Hawaii where 76 percent of the elderly population is Pacific/ Asian.

Statewide data revealed that 76 percent of the elderly 75 and over had one or more chronic conditons. However, 71 percent of the population between 65 and 74 also had chronic conditions. Further, when translated into actual numbers these percentages reflect about 14,000 age 75 and over and 27,000 age between ages 64 and 74. The young-old group outnumbering the old-old by 13,000. We should ask, then, whether using age 75 as a criterion will overlook many more in need. Furthermore, although the average life expectancy rate is expected to increase dramatically in the next twenty years, in Hawaii, where life expectancy is ranked the highest in the nation, it is 73.6 years. This is almost two years lower than the age criterion to be used by the human service model.

These data, then, although inadequate, point to the need to reassess the Subcommittee's proposal for giving first rights to those 75 years and older. Although the Subcommittee does indicate that "anyone slipping into functional dependence, even at an earlier age" would be served, using age 75 rather than functional dependence per se as the initial criterion would once again overlook most minority groups whose life expectancies are on the average shorter than their non-minority conterparts and who are less likely to be visible to the formal system of services. More equitable for Pacific/Asian elders, and minority elders in general, would be a policy based on functional dependence, regardless of chronological age. Data available provide evidence that chronic diseases and need for support services strike at varying ages; and, although their frequency increases with age, those under 75, particularly of minority groups, are also in need of comprehensive services.

If we are to focus on functional need, we must begin to develop more focussed research in the coming decade. At the forefront of our efforts should be the development of an equitable definition of "functional dependence," including not only physical limitaitons but availability of resources as well. We must obtain accurate national data regarding chronic conditons and their severity, economic and social resources, and physical and emotional health status of varying age and ethnic cohorts on a regular basis.

The options proposed by the Subcommittee are premature with the data at hand, and proceeding to implement such a proposal would be hazardous to the minority elderly. In order to address these issues we need—and do not have—data to answer the following questions on target groups and age-specific services: We need to know age-specific mortality and morbidity rates as well as the number and types of chronic conditions and limitations in activity with age for the varous Pacific/Asian subgroups. We also need data on differential rates not only by age but also by immigration wave and geographic locals. We also need more information on the multiple needs of these groups and what proportion are, in fact, using needed services. The discrepancy between need and service utilization has been corroborated by various studies in California and Washington, D.C. (Colen and Soto, Cuellar, Guttman, Ishizuka). However, we need more definitive information on the use of services in an age-integrated system vs. an age-segregated one. Colen and Soto found that programs exclusively for seniors or in which major components were earmarked for seniors were more likely to be successful in serving minority older persons than those who were integrated. We need to have these results corroborated on a large scale and in different locales across the country.

The proposed emphasis on prevention vs. treatment seems to conflict with the emphasis of the human service model on the functionally dependent population over 75. Nonetheless, prevention as a cornerstone of our aging policy is critically needed, particularly because of its long term impact on reducing frailty at later ages. To meet the needs of our Pacific/Asian elders adequately, it must take into account the variations in life styles, immigration experiences, cultural values and beliefs, and the support systems of our elders in terms of what does and does not contribute to their health and well-being. We need ethnic-specific and age-specific as well as generation-specific data on stress factors and nutritional patterns as well as longitudinal data to assess their effects over time. Of important in prevention are the behaviors and attitudes toward nutrition, health care, self-care and early detection. We can change unhealthful behaviors and conditions only if these elders are understood in this context. If prevention is to be effective, then more effort must be placed in obtaining ethnic-specific logitudinal data on factors related to wellbeing, and by indentifying behaviors and traditions which can be used to maintain and promote health and wellbeing in old age.

The type and scope of services proposed are two other issues which may negatively affect Pacific/Asian elders. At present there are no data on their utilization of either acute or long-term care facilities nor on other support services used by those who are frail. We need to examine the modes of coping with frailty by the formal system as well as by the informal family and neighborhood networks. One of the problems surfacing more visibly of late is that of the care of frail elderly family members. An unpublished study (Endo and Yoshida, 1968) of adult children of residents of Keiro Nursing Home in Los Angeles, indicated, the stresses of confronting the fact that one's parent had to be institutionalized and could not be cared for in one's own home. It is apparent, then, that we need to know more about not only the elders' needs for long-term care but the needs of their support networks as well.

In terms of the scope of services, we must first assess the impact of providing comprehensive services on the elder's independence. Does the provision of such assistance hinder or facilitate the person's independence? Further, if comprehensive services are to be provided for those elders 75 years and older only, would we be neglecting the preventive aspects of care and serving even less equitably our "young-old" Pacific/Asians, who are having difficulty at present obtaining the multiple services they need? Theequity in benefits studies in San Diego and Washington, D.C. indicate these multiple needs of our elders, ranging from housing, transportation to medical care. If these services are not provided when needed, but at a later time when the severity of problems negates their benefits, how will our elders fare? The one critical component which I find missing from the congressional Subcommittee's model for human services is the *human element*, i.e., those critical links between the client and the service.

The problem for the Asian/Pacific elderly—or, for the elderly in general, as I see it—is not the lack of services. The problem is that the Asian/Pacific elders are underutilizing these services. We even know the factors involved: lack of knowledge of services, inaccessibility to services, stigma of receiving services, lack of bilingual/bicultural staff. The critical question before us is not whether Asian and Pacific American elders have needs, but rather, how should programs be designed so as to enable them to use the services they need. After examining the various Asian/Pacific elderly monographs of the San Diego State University group, which included the Japanese, Chinese, Filipino, Guamanian, and Samoan elderly, I have found more similarities than dissimilarities in their attitudes toward utilizing services. I would thus posit that all ethnic groups have the same needs for income, health, housing, and transportation. The difference lies in the area of service delivery modes, i.e., informing elderly of services, getting them to use services they need, and getting them to modify services according to their preferences.

Studies conducted on needs and service utilization, have found consistently that the Pacific/Asian elderly underutilize services even when needs exist. More importantly, not only is information on services and benefits lacking, but even when services are known, they are reluctant to use services of the formal system. On the other hand, experiences of such ethnic-specific programs as On Lok, Koreisha and Kimochi nutrition programs, and UPAC's programs for Pacific/Asians in San Diego have demonstrated high participation by Pacific/Asian elders. A recent study of various elderly programs in California examined a number of factors important to success in service delivery to elderly Asian Americans (Colen and Soto, 1979). Of the 24 items identified, over 50 percent related to outreach and information dissemination through ethnic media and individuals. Other components that were critical were having staff who were sensitive to the needs of Asian clients as well as the site location within the community.

Examination of successful ethnic programs indicates that Pacific/Asian elderly do use services when they are in need, but several common denominators must be present:

1. They are located in the neighborhood, and are easily accessible to them;

2. They have an informal and personalized climate;

3. They have staff who are client-oriented, and who assist elders to get all the services needed;

4. They have bilingual and/or indigenous outreach workers who are concerned about the people and the community they serve, and are identified by the elderly as "knowledgeable friends" who can help.

The need for bilingual staff is even more critical for Pacific/Asian elderly. For example, among the Chinese and Japanese elderly 65 and over, more than 80 percent do not use English as their mother tongue.

Two other options which should not be overlooked in the Subcommittee's proposal deal with the administration and implementation of the human services system. The congressional intent and the new administration's inclinations all point to the decentralization of policymaking and service provision. Historically, the 60's saw the proliferation of federal categorical programs with hundreds of millions of dollars spent on social welfare and allied programs. Service delivery activities in the public sector increased but also blurred the private sector role in providing services—ultimately confusing the recipients of services. The 70's saw the administration's attempt to bring order through block grants and through efforts by states to reorganize programs to integrate the human services. However, these attempts have not been totally successful, perhaps due to the failure of those at the policy-making levels to develop a clear vision of what should comprise the human service system and to evaluate the existing service system. The same situation seems to be facing us today at a time when resources are even less available for human services. Although philosophically, a decentralized system seems most feasible in being most responsive to minority communities, we have yet to assess whether direct funding of ethnic-specific demonstration projects is more effective than ethnic-integrated services at the local level.

Here we can learn from our Pacific Jurisdiction colleagues who have been more successful in maintaining the cultural influence in their services. Perhaps becasue of the greater homogeneity of the communities within their jurisdictions, they have been able to serve their elders by requesting waivers to maintain intact their cultural traditions and extended family networks. However, because they do receive categorical grants from the Administration on Aging, certain regulations have prevented them from adequately servicing the unique needs of their elders.

The final option proposed by the Subcommittee is that of utilizing and developing private sector agencies and natural support groups rather than the public sector to deliver services. Although our data tell us that ethnic-based community agencies have been more successful in attracting ethnic elders to their programs, we have no data on whether these programs have been more cost-effective than public agencies in meeting elders' needs and in preventing dysfunction and premature institutionalization. We are beginning to obtain data—for example, On Lok has begun collecting a comprehensive file on all their clients—but we need more conclusive and comparable data from both private and public agencies.

We need to look at natural support systems. For elderly Asians and Pacific Islanders, the use of formal agencies outside the family and neighborhood is foreign. Whether it is the family or ethnic organization for Asians, the *matai* system for Samoans or the *ohana* for Hawaiians, these networks are significant supports to the older minority communities. We need to explore further the extent to which these social structures are used by our elderly to alleviate problems. We need to look also at the effect of current policies on this system, for example the SSI and Medicare regulations discouraging family care of the disabled, as well at the tolerance level of this system in providing for frail elders, i.e., at what point they break down, and what supports—fiscal and otherwise—can buttress this system.

In short, the Pacific/Asian community is beset with a myriad of questions with very little—and fragmented—data to produce conclusive answers for planning a future service system to deal equitably with our elders. What we do know is that our Pacific/Asian elders are more likely to have problems in meeting basic needs than their non-minority counterparts, that they are heterogeneous, and that, although they have needs, they are less likely to know of services and to use them. In conclusion, the data consistently tell us that our Pacific/Asian elders have multiple needs, the most critical being access to services and benefits as well as the need for service deliverers to be sensitive to their cultural and language needs. Thus, if the focus of aging policy will be on the 75 and older population, it will neglect our elders who have only recently adjusted to using services heretofore available and accessible to all elders.

The policy shift posited by the Subcommittee on Human Services assumes that the Aging Network has done so well in mainstreaming our elders that they will be able to obtain all services they need in the adult service system. Although fragmentary, our data just do not bear this out—our Pacific/Asian elders have difficulty accessing needed services even in the age-specific system. What is needed in the aging policy for the future is a greater emphasis on linking needy elders to services. At the same time, we should not lose sight of advocating on behalf of all elders to improve their quality of life, including such preventive activities as nutrition, socialization, transportation, etc. If this is to be accomplished, the human service system must be based on a more accurate and longitudinal data on all elderly—and this means identifying our Pacific/Asian subpopulations by not merely including them as "non-whites"—or "all others"; and it must sensitize service deliverers to cultural variations in implementing an equitable and effective service delivery system.

Sylvia Yuen Schwitters, Ph.D.
Department of Human Development
University of Hawaii

RESEARCH ON PACIFIC/ASIAN ELDERS

There are two major difficulties in discussing research issues relating to Pacific/Asian elders. One pertains to the inherent diversity of the population. Elder Pacific/Asians include: Native-American Hawaiians and recent Indo-Chinese refugees; first-generation Issei from Japan and American-born, third-generation Sansei; Samoans sharing the same household with a myriad of family members and relatives; single Filipino men living alone in boarding houses; college-educated Chinese and illiterate Chinese. Among the broad spectrum of people are the commonly acknowledged (Pacific/Asian Elderly Research Project, 1978b) variations in language, values, traditions and history, and the less-frequently cited (Schwitters & Ashdown, 1981; Schwitters & Tomita, 1981) differences in life expectancy and health. For this reason, advancing recommendations regarding an optimum human service model requires extreme caution, for what may be appropriate for one subset of Pacific/Asians may miss the mark for anothrer.

The other difficulty relates to the body of research knowledge in the area. The present state of the literature has been described (Pacific/Asian Elderly Research Project, 1978c) as descriptive and impressionistic, limited to small samples and specific areas, and with national, cross-sectional and cross-cultural studies virtually non-existent. Elsewhere in this issue, the directors of the Minority Aging Codification Project report that there is less documentation relating to Pacific/Asians that there is for blacks and Hispanic Americans. Further, the majority of the materials consists of unpublished papers, conference proceedings, and reports, rather than articles in referred journals. Although it is easy to criticize much of the existing literature and to decry the dearth of documents based on well-designed studies with valid and reliable data, it is more realistic to acknowledge that the research on Pacific/Asian elders is in its infancy. Investigations focussed on minority elders began in the sixties, while interest in Pacific/Asians in particular developed in the seventies. The effect of federal funds for minority aging research and training, intially granted during the early 1970s, was not manifested until the latter part of that decade. Therefore, it is not surprising that, like all other new fields, research on Pacific/Asian elders presently lacks the rigor, sophistication and quantification that should be forthcoming in the years ahead.

This is not to say that substantial gains have not been made in the field. There is, for example, a respectable body of information (Cuellar & Weeks, 1980; Colen & Sot, 1979; Federal Council on Aging, 1979; Pacific/Asian Elderly Research Project, 1978a) now available regarding both the barriers to services and resources that elderly Pacific/Asians confront and the components essential to culturally relevant programs. The barriers include lack of English proficiency, lack of knowledge concerning resources and how to gain access to them, lack of transportation, the location of services outside of minority communities, and cultural values that are at odds with seeking and receiving public benefits. The components for success encompass the presence of bilingual/bicultural workers in multiservice senior centers, based in minority communities, which employ Pacific/Asian elders in the planning process and which have an effective outreach system.

Given what is known, where should future research be directed in order to provide the body of knowledge necessary to address policy issues regarding the aged? Four critical domains in which research data are notably absent are identified below. Without advances in these areas, questions regarding service priorities—including those posed by the human service model proposed by the Select Committee on Aging—can only be answered partially or with too many assumptions and too few facts.

Need for Inclusionary Research

Although other writers have called for separate assessments of the health, economic wellbeing, and housing conditons of elderly Pacific/Asians—similar to those recently commissioned for the other three major minority groups—this writer believes inclusion in ongoing national assessments is the better route to follow. It cannot be stated emphatically enough that ethnic minorities, particularly American Indians, Hispanic Americans, and Pacific/Asians, have been ignored and treated as non-persons in the information gathering and reports on the old. In virtually all surveys on older people in the United States—among them the Annual Housing Survey by the Department of Housing and Urban Development and the various health surveys by the National Center for Health Statistics—Pacific/Asians are noticeably absent. The problem of omission begins in the initial design of inventories when race/ethnicity is only defined as white and other, white and black, or at most, white, black, and other. All of these categories clump non-white people together and are insensitive to the heterogeneity among minority group elders. During the data collection stage, Pacific/Asians tend to be excluded and undercounted becasue most investigations do not utilize the outreach methods and bilingual, culturally sensitive interviewers necessary to obtain their input. When baseline information is not available on selected subgroups of the population, their status is not presented in reports by governmental bodies (e.g., Federal Council on Aging, 1981; President's Commission on Mental Health: Task Panel on the Elderly & Secretary's Committee on Mental Health and Illness of the Elderly, 1980), textbooks, journal articles, and other documents on the aged. As a consequence, lawmakers, policy formulators, scholars and the general public may not be aware that their perceptions of older people are shaped as much by the absence, as by the presence of information. In such a context, elderly Pacific/Asians are frequently stereotyped as problem-free because there are no solid, convincing data to document need; if evidence can be demonstrated at the local level, it is insufficent to have major impact in the determination of national policies, programs and funds.

A parallel system of assessing the status and needs of minority older people is too dependent on the political climate, availability of special funds, and other shifting conditions. An integrated, inclusionary system—one in which Pacific/Asian elders are included in ongoing national—surveys offers the advantages of consistency over time, comparability with other ethnic groups, and currency of information. Admittedly, the small number of Pacific/Asians in comparison to the total United States population will require procedures and expenditures beyond present levels, such as over-sampling to insure sufficient numbers of subjects for data analyses and the translation of protocols. However, such actions are long overdue and are a necessary process in the full recognition and equitable treatment of all of this nation's people.

Need for Macro-level Research

The vast majority of the literature on elderly Pacific/Asians describes the history, problems, and special concerns of this group. Although individual and specific group percpectives assist in understanding the present cohort of elders, macro-level research provides the means through which qualititave changes can be made in people's lives. What is suggested here is a greater emphasis on approaching the problems confronting minority aged by examining the impact of state and federal legislation, policies, and regulations. For example, compared to the majority population, Pacific/Asians have a lower mean income and a higher percentage of individuals below the poverty level, a status that persists into old age (Benedict, 1978). Despite their economic conditon, Pacific/Asians tend to be underserved in terms of resources and services for the old. Guttman (1980) reported that Asian elders were over-represented among those with no knowledge of public benefits, encoutered more problems in seeking assistance than did blacks or whites, and differed significantly from other minorities with regard to feelings that prevented them from seeking assistance. For these reasons, among those in need, the Asians in Guttman's sample had the highest percentage of individuals who did not seek aid (43 percent vs. 26 percent for blacks, 33 percent for HIspanic Americans, and 12 percent for whites). The aged who do not live in high=density minority areas are particularly prone to have their needs go unrecognized and unattended. In a survey of community-based services in long-term care, Holmes and his colleagues (1979) found that only 16 of 62 agencies (27 percent) in counties with an Asian population served any members of that ethnic group. Most (N = 34, 74 percent) of the agencies serving no Asians were located in communities where they constituted only 1 to 3 percent of the population.

Thus, there is good reason to explore the means in which economic benefits can be transferred directly to minority aged, rather than transmitted in the form of public services which elderly Pacific/Asians are reluctant to utilize and for whom access is difficult. Tax credits for senior citizens, changes in social security benefits, reduction formulae in the tax rates of older workers, and other proposals with long-term economic consequences have been advanced. There is, however, little or no information regarding how any of these measures will affect elderly Pacific/Asians in general, and specific segments of that population in particular.

Need for Culturally Appropriate Instruments

Because much of the work in the field has been based on observations, subjective accounts, and descriptions of phenomena using relatively small samples of respondents, appropriate assessment tools have not been an especially critical problem to date. In the future, however, research on elderly Pacific/Asians will expand to include more than one cohort within an ethnic group, subjects from several ethnic groups and/or countries in areas which require sophisticated measuring devices. Mistranslations in word and concept are obvious errors to be avoided, amusing though they may sometimes be. "Come alive with Pepsi" provoked different responses from Americans and Germans when it was translated in German to "Come Alive out of the Grave with Pepsi"; elsewhere the slogan was translated: "Pepsi Brings your Ancestors Back from the Grave" (Time, 1981).

Less obvious errors are the culturally-evoked responses, such as mood states, verbal responses, and behaviors, which may be weighted or interpreted in a way that skewd results. In addition, what is not measured may also distort the findings. Using culturally inappropriate inventories, an investigator may determine that a sample of elderly Korean women tend to be passive and dependent, when in reality they may have far more aggressive, independent and controlling impulses than indicated, but simply manifest them in different ways than were measured.

The Need for An Explication of "Cultural Sensitivity"

The importance of cultural sensitivity in the delivery of services to aged minorities is a generally accepted premise upon which is based recommendations for ethnic specific services and contracts to minority organizations (Cuellar & Weeks, 1980; Colen & Soto, 1979). While it may be true that elderly Pacific/Asians are attracted to services with providers of their own ethnic backgrounds and underutilize services without them, a fundamental research task is to define the basic elements that constitute the reason for program success. What qualities do these ethnic minority staff members possess? Are bilingual ability, good listening skills, knowledge of cultural values and traditions, the ability to empathize, and/or other traits essential in the cluster of factors which make up cultural sensitivity? Once these core characteristics have been identified, the following question should be asked: Can the qualities comprising cultural sensitivity be taught to others and can they be evaluated? The importance of these actions lies in their potential to provide tools that can be used to predict, transfer, and evaluate a heretofore nebulous variable. If cultural sensitivity can be predicted, then program directors will be assisted in screening and selecting applicants who have the greatest probability of performing well with Pacific/Asian older people. If cultural sensitivity can be transferred, then individuals without it or with lesser quantities of it can be taught to relate more competently and effectively with aged Pacific/Asians. And if cultural sensitivity can be evaluated, there will be an objective means available by which staff can be assessed in the performance toward the attainment of program goals.

Research conducted in the explication of cultural sensitivity may make the choice between ethnic specific or ethnic integrated services irrelevant, and suggest it was never the right question. Research data in this area will provide ethnic minority advocates a firmer base to advance their demand that cultural sensitivity be an essential component in *all* programs for the aged. Insensitivity to culturally different clients no longer need to be tolerated regardless of the numbers they represent in the community and the ethnic composition of service providers. This position does force an evaluation of previously held beliefs which were difficult to defend. For example, if the aged and programs must be ethnically matched for optimum services, is there not a form of discrimination operating against Pacific/Asians when their resource options are reduced? Furthermore, why do some ethnically different staff memebers work better with elders than do staff of the same ethnicity? Disquieting though the examination can be, it creates new and exciting opportunities. For ethnic researchers and service providers, the arena for their expertise in the transfer of knowledge pertaining to cultural sensitivity—in development, training, and evaluation—will be expanded to all aging programs, rather than limited to those that are minority focused. Perhaps the greatest contribution of all will be the freedom of elderly Pacific/Asians to select the services they desire and to be assured that they will be served as adequately as majority group people.

In 1970 there were 1.5 million Pacific/Asian individuals in the United States. A decade later their numbers had increased to 3.5 million—a growth rate of 128 percent, higher than that of the majority or of any other minority group in the nation—and the sharp expansion is expected to continue in the years ahead. Elderly Pacific/Asians are expected to increase at an even faster rate than their younger cohorts, a prediction that is based on the aging of the relatively "young" Pacific/Asian population, their increased life expectancy, and the addition of recent elderly immigrants (sponsored into the United States by children and relatives). The changes wrought by demography and time will result in greater diversity and modifications in the composition of this group. The term Pacific/Asian will be stretched to cover fourth and fifth generation, highly educated individuals who are well assimilated into the majority group, economically secure, and knowledgeable about dealing with the bureaucratic system, as well as recent non-English speaking immigrants with little education and few technical skills, who feel more comfortable living a traditional lifestyle largely within minority enclaves. The preponderance of elderly men in some ethnic groups will disappear, and there will be more elderly women among all Pacific/Asian groups than at the present time. The Filipinos and Indo-Chinese will constitute larger proportions of the total Pacific/Asian population, resulting in corresponding reductions in some of the other ethnic groups.

How can Pacific/Asian advocates meet the challenges of an evolving constituency within a rapidly changing society? Although research can probably never provide *the* answer, it can be used to assist in providing directions and making more enlightened choices. Research on elderly Pacific/Asians is in its early stages, and like most growing things, if well nurtured it can take a form that will provide many benefits in the future. Careful attention to the areas of inclusionary research, macro-level research, research on culturally relevant instruments, and reserach explicating cultural sensitivity will yield especially great rewards.

References

Benedict, R. Federal policies and the minority elders. In E. Percil Stanford (Ed.) *Retirement: Concepts and realities.* San Diego, California: University Center on Aging, San Diego State University, 1978.

Colen, J.N. *Service delivery to aged minorities: Techniques of successful programs.* Sacramento, California: California State University School of Social Work, 1979.

Cuellar, J.B., & Weeks, J. *Minority elderly Americans: A prototype for area agencies on aging.* San Diego, California: Allied Home Health Association, 1980.

Federal Council on Aging. *Policy Issues concerning the elder minorities.* Washington, D.C.: DHHS Publication No. (OHDS) 80-20670, 1980.

Federal Council in Aging. *The need for long term care: Information and issues.* Washington, D.C.: DHHS Publication No. (OHDS) 81-21704, 1981.

Guttmann, D. *Perspective on equitable share in public benefits by minority elderly.* Washington, D.C.: The Catholic University of America, 1980.

Holmes, D., Holmes, M., Steinbach, L., Hausner, T., and Rocheleau, B. The use of community-based services in long-term care by older minority persons. *The Gerontologist, 1979, 19(4)*, 389-397.

"Oops! How's that again? *Time,* March 30, 1981, pp. 85-86.

Pacific/Asian Elderly Research Project. *Critical factors in service delivery,* 1978a.

Pacific/Asian Elderly Research Project. *Working paper: Preliminary framework for service delivery model building,* May, 1978b.

Pacific/Asian Elderly Research Project. *Working paper on unmet research needs in the Pacific/Asian elderly community,* March, 1978c.

President's Commission on Mental Health: Task Panel on the Elderly & Secretary's Committee on the Mental Health and Illness of the Elderly. *Mental health and the elderly: Recommendations for action.* Washington, D.C.: DHEW Publication No. (OHDS) 80-20960, 1980.

Schwitters, S., & Ashdown. Elderly Hawaiians in a changing society. *Aging,* April-May, 1981.

Schwitters, S., & Tomita, S. *Differences in health status among minority elderly in Hawaii.* Paper presented at the Western Gerontological Society 27th Annual Meeting, Seattle, Washington, April 11-15, 1981.

III

Strategies for Impacting the Older Americans Act

Esther Jones Langston, Ph.D.
University of Nevada at Las Vegas

MODELS FOR LINKING FORMAL AND INFORMAL NETWORKS: IMPLICATIONS FOR POLICIES AND PROGRAMS

The Older Americans Act created in 1965 the Administration on Aging, putting into law one of the most radical pieces of social legislation in the history of this country. One of the most significant and liberal aspects of the act is its universalism of coverage. Under this social policy, recipients may acquire services merely on the basis of demand, without regard to their economic status.

The titles of the act include a range of service provisions. Title I outlines the objectives of the act, which essentially are to provide the best quality of life available through support of research on the needs of elders, and attention to effective and efficient service delivery to them. It is under this title that the values, norms and customs are reflected. Through the focus of this title of the act on the nature and interaction of social forces, the United States government communicates its perception and value of the elderly as members of this society.

The Administration on Aging is established under Title II, which spells out cleary its authority and range of responsibility. Under the Commissioner on Aging, who is appointed by the President and the Senate, the administration is designated the primary agency for carrying out the act. The functions of the administration range from serving as a clearinghouse for information related to problems of the aging and aged to the development of a national plan for meeting the needs for trained personnel in the field of aging. Towards these ends, the administration operates the National Information and Resource Clearing House for the Aging and the Federal Council on Aging. The powers in this organization control the type, nature and extent of information that will be disseminated about the aged on a national level. The Federal Council on Aging serves as the advisor to the president on matters related to the special needs of older Americans and assists the commissioner in making the appraisal of needs.

Title III, Grants for State and Community Programs on Aging, intends to encourage and assist state and local agencies in concentrating their resources for the development of comprehensive and coordinated service systems to serve older individuals. To this end, it fosters new cooperative arrangements with state and local agencies, and with the providers of social servies, including nutrition services and multipurpose senior centers. Part B of this title authorizes grants to states under state plans to provide an array of social services. Part C specifically provides for nutritional services, both congregate and home-delivered. Part C is geared to discretionary programs and projects such as demonstration projects like alternative health-care delivery systems, advocacy and outreach programs and transportation services. Part D addresses mortgage insurance and interest grants for multipurpose senior centers. The purpose of this segment is to assist and encourage the provision of needed facilities for elderly programs.

Training and Research are the foci of Title IV. The purpose of this title is to enhance the quality of services by maintaining a steady supply of adequately trained personnel in the field of aging. Without personnel training programs there would be a tremendous shortage of aging professionals to meet the increasing demands of the elderly. In order to monitor the personnel needs in the field, Title IV finances programs that will: 1) develop information on the actual needs for personnel to work in the field of aging, both present and long-range; 2) provide a broad range of quality training and retraining opportunities; 3) attract a greater number of qualified persons into the field; and 4) help to make training programs more responsive to the needs in the field of aging.

Title V, Community Services Employment, is directed to develop alternatives for innovative work modes and to provide technical assistance in creating job opportunities via work-sharing and other experiential methods to prime sponsors, labor organizations and groups representing business and industry. This title is based heavily on cooperative agreements or relationships with private industry as well as the public sector. Part B of this title is devoted to fostering and promoting useful part-time opportunities in community service activities for unemployed, low-income individuals 55 years of age and older. This segment of the title provides a means of enhancing employment opportunities for those low-income persons with poor employment prospects.

A major addition to the act is Title VI, which is designated as provider of Grants for Indian Tribes. The essence of this title is the provision of comprehensive social and nutritional services for Indians, comparable to the services provided for under Title III. The feasibility of this title has been questioned in view of the comprehensiveness of Title III. In addition, it has been called superfluous, since Title III cites priority to the low-income, minority and frail elderly. Defenders of Title VI argue that the historical circumstances which disenfranchised the American Indian justify the need for both separate and inclusive coverage to assure adequate respoonse to their plight.

These titles represent various segments of social policy regarding the life circumstances of the elderly. To the extent that the programs and services outlined under this legislation constitute how the circumstances of the elderly are defined and responded to, they do provide a comprehensive service system. Therefore, in order to meet these ever-increasing demands of social service delivery for the aged, it is necessary that various aspects of the current social service system be scrutinized to determine its effectiveness.

As defined in the Older Americans Act, the problem of age is seen as primarily one of the fragmentation of services. The paradigm implicit in this definition limits the scope of individual efforts, emphasizing instead planning, coordination and pooling of resources to create comprehensive service systems. The vagueness and ambiguity implicit in such terms as planning and pooling has given different interest groups and professionals the opportunity to redefine the solution as falling within their own special domains. In this process, the aged are perceived as dependent and in need of special services prescribed and provided largely by the professionals (Estes, 1975: 5).

Existing institutional and power relationships are maintained by a policy paradigm that imposes problem definitions that in turn legitimize reorgainization through coordination of existing services. The inherent contradiction of such a program is that it cannot solve the problems of the aged because it never addresses them. The vague mandates which constrict programs and measures appropriations of the Older Americans Act have resulted in services that reach only a small percentage of the elderly. The contrast between the sweeping objectives of Older Americans Act and the limited authority provided to the Administration on Aging and the other agencies created and supported under the act, points to its the symbolic nature. This symbolism is not inconsequential, however, in that it generates rising expectations and demands which expand the resource base of organizational service providers, while simultaneously confusing the public and most importantly the aged themselves as to the realistic potential for American social policy to alter their social status and include their conditions (Estes, 1976:6).

Policies based on the symbolic interaction framework take an optimistic view of the aged. This view does not identify particular behavior, activity patterns, or experience with old age, but rather emphasizes the social construction of these in light of interpretive and negotiated interactional encounters. Because symbolic interactionism focuses on both environment and individual, one policy emphasis might be the interventions that seek to modify environmental constraints and another on those directed to the needs of the individuals (Estes, 1979:9).

Older persons, especially minority elderly, are powerless to alter their social status and conditions because their problems and appropriate remedies are socially defined, largely by the dominant members of the society. Since the label and definitions apply to any group in society, reciprocal relationships in which relative power, class and social standards are the interactions played upon the aged cannot unilaterally alter their relationships to the rest of society (Estes, 1979:5).

The implications and program presented in this paper address some of the concerns which affect the formulation of policies and the implementations of programs and delivery of service to the black aged. The focus is on developing policies and programs which modify the environment constraints and also meet the needs of the black aged in American society.

Models for Providing Services

Several recent policy statements have focussed upon the relationship between formal sources of help provided by professional service agencies and the informal helping sources to which many of us turn in everyday life. (President's Commission on Mental Health, 1978; Strengthening Families Through Informal Support System, 1979; National Commission on Neighborhoods, 1979). In the concern for assuring that citizens have a comprehensive range of formal services available to help them in times of need or with specific problems, the fact that informal helping resources may also be available and appropriate has often been overlooked. Neighbors, friends, storekeepers, ministers, not to mention family members, all have important helping roles to play. The task for public policy is to understand how formal and informal sources of help can interact synergistically rather than destructively.

The models presented in this paper were modified from research conducted at the Regional Research Institute at Portland State University by Charles Froland, Diane Pancost, Nancy Chapman, and Priscilla Kimboko. Their research was based on the study of ten programs which developed different ways of linking formal services with informal helping networks.

Research Approach

The research underlying these models began with an ideal model that included definitions of what was meant by formal services and by helping networks and hypotheses about the nature of the interactions between the two. In general, formal services were seen as agencies employing professional staff, with an operational program of services oriented to human service objectives. This study focussed on informal helping networks.

A helping network was generally expected to be a set of relationships between people who were performing informal helping roles and other individuals linked to helpers by neighborhood proximity, personal acquaintance or common concern. Relationships were expected to have arisen spontaneously, in a setting not necessarily connected with the agency, with informal exchanges of help and assistance freely given and based on mutuality. The interaction between the agency and such a helping network was expected to have several key attributes. Agency staff were expected to have an explicit methodology or set of criteria by which they identified helping networks to interact with the informal helpers as equals, and to be sensitive to ethnic and cultural values. The intent of intervention was expected to be directed to reaching a broader group of individuals through the helping network than could be reached in the typical casework approach.

The researchers were also interested in understanding how the concept of linking formal and informal helpers could be extended to different types of problems, agency settings and community contexts. This approach brought the traditional split between theory and practice into the picture, as it soon became clear that ideal expectations were not possible or appropriate in all circumstances. The realization that neighborhoods were not relevant to some problems, that networks differed in form and function according to situational exigencies, and that many agencies were involved in an exploratory and developmental endeavor which resulted in dramatic changes over time in what they were doing and how they conceptualized it, led to some need to relax the formal requirements of the study. Programs were selected that came as close as possible to meeting sample expectations, with the ten programs providing a basis to define a larger sample for study later in the research.

The programs were found in several contexts which ranged from sparsely-settled rural areas to deteriorated inner cities. Some were operating in areas with strong local identity and a high level of interaction. Others were found in areas with little or no neighborhood identy, although most of the areas did have stable populatons. Some programs were not neighborhood-based at all and related instead to a dispersed population with a common problem or need.

The agencies involved in these programs exhibited some variation but also had some common elements. None of them were large state or federal agencies such as public welfare agencies. Some programs were undertaken explicitly as demonstration or research projects while others represented the outgrowth of an attempt by an agency to develop a better relationship with an area or target population, sometimes at the demand of the client group. No program had been in operation longer than six years and most were less than four years old. All of the programs were small, with from two to nine staff members.

The ten programs in the sample served a range of target populations: three serving the elderly, two serving children, youth and families, one serving developmentally disabled and four serving the general community.

Factors to Consider Linking Formal and Informal Services

Factors such as the types of problems and client populations each agency works with, the stability of the neighborhood or community in which clients live, the legal and political climate encountered by the agency, the agency's organizational base and the personalities of the staff and informal helpers all serve to influence the various directions that may be pursued in lining the efforts of professional staff and informal helpers. Despite this adversity, having a common philosophy insures some comparability.

Characteristics of Helping Networks

The kinds of helping networks with which staff are linked vary according to the different objectives ov the programs. The staff have reasons for seeking informal sources of help, and these reasons have major influences on the way they define and identify a helping network. There are several possibilities to this approach. Some programs may focus exclusively on a given client, e.g., an elderly widow, and the primary concern is to identify the personal support network of that individual. Staff may draw upon outside support resources when the existing personal network of a client is limited or not supportive. In these instances, the boundaries of the helping network are largely tied to an individual client, although more group-oriented helping may occur.

Another possibility is a focus on the needs of a population group that is concerned with promoting mutual-aids or self-help networks within that group. Informal mutual aids groups share similarities with the helping that occurs within organized self-help groups in that individuals come together on the basis of shared problems or circumstances (Katz and Bender, 1976). The important diference is that the informal helping that transpires within the mutual aid network is free of the influences of formal charger and organization that characterize many self-help groups. Helping is more dependent on maintaining norms of reciprocity than on supporting a group identity or organizational philosophy.

Another focus is on geographical propinquity. This focus may be used when program objectives are difected to community-wide issues or to populations clearly identifies with a defined locality. Programs adopting this perspective identify key figures within neighborhood areas, people who perform central helping roles, so called "natural helpers" (Collins and Pancoast, 1976). For example, a program serving the elderly identifies natural helpers who are instrumental in looking after a large number of elderly individuals by providing emotional support and assistance with shopping, meals, or transportation, etc. Another program responsible for housing assistance and community development identifies neighborhood-based lay facilitators who provide information, advice and referral to residents regarding public services.

Some programs may have identified existing, locality-based helping networks; others have to foster them. For programs concerned with creating community networks, various types of community representatives have been identified, such as school officials, clergy, storekeepers or simply knowledgeable residents who are then organized into helping networks by program staff.

Table 1 summarizes the variety of helping networks that staff of the ten programs have enlisted in their work. The examples are classified according to three different bases for defining a network, i.e., individual, population group, or locality, as well as whether the network exists independent of the program or whether the program played a role in creating the network.

Table 1.
Types of Helping Networks

| Basis | Source | |
	Existing	Created
Individual	personal network of individual client	linking helper to individual client
Population	mutual aid network	linking similar individuals for mutual aid
Locality	central figures in neigborhood network	organizing community representatives

These various forms of informal helping networks, whether based on personal support needs, mutual aid or on a particular locality, are only three instances of the more encompassing phenomenon of informal helping. What distinguishes this set of examples is the active involvement, in a planned way, of agency personnel with informal helpers and helping activities. This approach is provided as a guide for identifying informal helping networks.

Types of Relationships

The relationship between staff professionals and informal helpers is an important element in the way helping networks are identified or created, determining both the types of help exchanged and the purpose and meaning of such exchanges. The variety of relationships developed is a result of the different personalities, backgrounds and cultures of the staff of the programs and the helping networks with which they are involved. These relationships can be classified by examining the postures that professional staff adopt when working with informal helpers.

Professional helping is often based on standards of training and experience; knowledge and expertise are valued in establishing the credibility of the help provided. For informal helpers, these standards may have little meaning, as helping may be based on informal personal relationships, shared experiences and altruism, with credibility more dependent on the norms of exchange within the network. Both types of helping have value; the realtionship formed between the two must acknowledge the value of each type while coming to terms with issues involving differences in responsibility, authority and status.

Three different types of relationships seem to characterize the range of orientations professional staff and informal helpers may adopt. These may be termed collegial, coordinative and directive. A *collegial* relationship between staff and helpers is characterized by mutual independence; each respects the other and each determines what their tasks of helping are to be. Staff often provide support and consultation to helpers as colleagues. A program that works with kin, friends and neighbors of an elderly client is illustrative of this type of relationship on which staff periodically call up significant helpers within the client's personal network to ask how things are going, whether any assistance is needed, and to support what the helper has been doing. A *coordinative* relationship retains many of the informal features of a collegial relationship in that staff and helpers perform separate functions with equal authority. However, as the name implies, staff coordinate or organize many of the helpers' activities in accomplishing various tasks. For example, staff of a program in San Antonio which is concerned with elderly Mexican Americans have organized task forces of natural helpers to provide services to their elderly neighbors. Individual helpers make their own decisions about the help they provide, but staff coordinate the activities of several helpers to provide a full range of services from home maintenance to social and healthe service.

In the last type of relationship, *directive*, staff assume a more supervisory role in working with helpers. Staff identify individuals who are particularly knowledgeable or skillful with respect to some aspect of identified needs, e.g., (independent living), managing the attendants who provide care, and recruit persons and provide training to meat the client's identified needs. Although many aspect of the realtionships between the staff and the helpers are non-directive, staff both decide the skill areas in which helpers are to provide care and specify how training should be provided. In these respects, they play a more directive role in the range of tasks informal helpers are to perform.

The three types of relationships presented above were compared along six dimensions of interaction between staff and helper—focus, formality, organization, training, type of helping exchange and expected duration of the relationship. These dimensions are defined as follows:

focus—whether the objectives of the interaction are primarily directed to client problems or community issues;

formality—whether formal titles or explicit role definitions are employed (formal) or whether helper's roles are defined more informally;

organization—whether staff interact with helpers primarily on a one-to-one basis or in a group;

training—whether a formal or structured training program is offered to helpers, informal training occurs in helping activities or no training is provided to helpers;

type of helping exchange—whether the help provided by helpers is more effective (involving exchanges of emotional support, advice or information) or is instrumental (involving exchanges of resources such as transportation or yard work and task focussed activity such as program development or community organizing);

expected duration—whether there is an expectation that the realtionship between staff and helpers is open and may continue indefinitely, or whether the relationship is more time limited and will end upon the completion of a task or resolution of a particular problem.

Table 2.

Dimensions of Relationships Between Formal and Informal Helpers*

| | Type of Relationship | | |
	Collegial	Coordinative	Directive
Focus			
Client	4	3	2
Community	0	5	0
Formality			
Formal	0	2	2
Informal	4	6	0
Organization			
One-to-one	3	1	1
Group	1	7	1
Training			
Formal	0	1	1
Informal	0	5	0
None	4	2	1
Type of Help			
Affective	4	2	1
Instrumental	0	6	1
Expected Duration			
Limited	1	7	2
Open	3	1	0

*Note: Figures based on staff-helper interaction among fourteen different helping networks across the ten programs.

Table 2 highlights several differences among the types of relationships developed between staff and helping networks. Most "collegial" relationships are shown to be focussed on client-oriented objectives which involve effective exchanges of help. Helping roles are not formally defined, no training is provided helpers and staff generally relate to helpers on a one-to-one basis with the duration of the relationship being more open-ended. In contrast, a coordinative type of relationship is usually focussed on community level issues and involves more instrumental exhanges of help or assistance. Staff and helper relate informally on a group basis, informal training is usually provided and relationships are expected to be more time limited in duration.

A Typology of Agency Approaches

Table 3.

A Typology of Approaches for Working with Informal Helping Networks

Approach	Focus	Source	Relationship	Objectives
Personal Network	Individual	Existing	Collegial	Strengthen existing support
Volunteer Linking	Individual	Created	Directive	Develop support system social integration
Mutual Aid Network	Population group	Existing/ created	Coordinative	Promote sharing and support of mutual problems
Neighborhood Helpers	Locality	Existing	Collegial	Strengthen neighborhood self-help
Community Empowerment	Locality	Created	Coordinative	Build community capacity for problem solving

Personal Network Intervention

This approach focuses on existing relationships of an individual client. Agency staff develop collegial relationships with kin, friends, or neighbors who are significant in providing help to a client. In this approach, staff identify helpers within the client's network and provide support and consultation to affirm and sustain this resource for a client. The data in this study indicate a high justification for this approach in providing services to the black aged.

Volunteer Linking

This approach also focuses on a client's personal network but is concerned with augmenting or creating additional helping resources for a client. The approach involves a more directive stance on the part of the agency staff, in which informal helpers are recruited, sometimes trained, to provide support or assistance to a client.

Mutual Aid Networks

This approach adopts a focus on a client populations experiencing similar problems, stressful experiences of circumstances and involves collaborating with an existing self-help group or alternatively creating a network among a group of clients. Relationships may be more collegial when the mutual aid group has been established without staff effort with a more coordinative relationship characteristic of staff-created groups, e.g., (a program working with senior citizens may develop a relationship with a senior social activites group as a way to reduce social isolation among the elderly.) Group members may provide transportation assistance, help with shopping as well as outreach to elderly clients. Based on the data in this research, this approach has great benefits to the rural black elderly.

Neighborhood Helpers

With focus on a particular geographical locality, this approach usually involves canvassing a neighborhood to identify "natural helpers" within existing helping networks with staff attempting to form collegial realtionships and to strengthen or support the role of the natural helpers. A senior center situated in a neighborhood with a high number of elderly citizens may develop a resource file of neighborhood helpers who have provided assistance to elderly residents and others. Staff members consult with these helpers and may call upon them when someone in the neighborhood needs help. The data in this study, indicates taht 328 of the 487 respondents know their neighbors as personal friends, which indicates that this approach has a high utility in providing an effective service delivery system to the black aged.

Community Empowerment

Similar in focus to the neighborhood helping approach, the community empowerment approach shifts attention to creating or organizing helping networks among community residents in order to develop a "community voice" or build a community's capacity for self help.

These five approaches have certain implications for how professional activities should be keyed to the needs of particular informal modes of helping. One thing that emerges from the comparisons is a certain concordance of the character of the relationship developed between staff and helpers and the source of the helping network, i.e. whether it was preexisting or created in response to the program.

In none of the instances where the helping network was created by the activities of the agency's program could the character of the relationship between staff and helpers be considered collegial. This type of relationship occurs exclusively with preexisting networks. However, for some preexisting populations or locality-based helping networks, staff have developed coordinative relationships. This usually has occurred where the nature of the helping exchange is task-oriented, involving program development or community organizing objectives.

The association between existing and created networks and the type of staff/helper relationship has an intuitive explanation. An established network of helping relationships carries with it implicit expectations or norms; professional staff are essentially outsiders who must adapt or integrate themselves within such a network. This is best done when the approach is collegial and respectful of established helping roles and activities. Where staff play a more active role in fostering the development of a helping network, they also have more opportunity for structuring or directing the helping network; this is supported by the preponderance of coordinative or directive relationships associated with the helping networks created by staff within the ten programs researched.

The typology may offer a way to conceptualize these approaches so that other issues of practice and policy may be more clearly understood. While this typology is based on empirical evidence from a limited number of program, it resembles those developed by several authors based on literature reviews and thus has more general application (Gottlieb, 1979; Erickson, 1975; Pilisuk, Chandler and D'Onofrio, 1978; Schon, 1977; Froland, 1979).

Issues for Policy and Practice

In the course of studying the ten programs, a number of more general issues have also emerged which bear on policy and practice. These issues ccan be stated briefly as questions to highlight some of the dilemmas that may be faced by formal agency staff in their program development.

Staff Role

How do staff personnel accomodate professional identities, norms and values to helpers who do not have a professional perspective? In some instances, there may be differences in assumptions and interests between professionals as they view their work and helpers whose views are more related to the informal network within which they are embedded. Sometimes this tension may be dealt with by procedures of staff recruitment and training although value differences may persist. There can be an attitude of equal status when one party may consider knowledge, skills and training to establish the legitimacy of helping while the other relies on friendship and mutual aid in providing help.

Agency Organization

There are several ways in which being part of a formal organization may raise issues for staff. First, funding sources and demands for accountability often either impose requirements for documentation which may prove disruptive or eligibility rules which may create arbitrary limits in working with informal helping networks. Second a greater degree of organizational complexity and specialization often provides barriers to a free flow of communication or mitigates against the close personal relationships that are part of working with networks. Finally, whether staff members consider themselves representatives of a formal organization or more-or-less-free agents will alter their relationships to a helping network or perhaps determine the type of network they may enlist in their work.

Helper Role

The issue of what a "natural" helper is or becomes in the context of working with staff of a formal service agency raises several questions. First, how much does the process of formalizing the helper's role automatically occur in the course of realating to a formal agency, and are the consequences of formalization positive or negative? Some agencies seem particularly concerned with maintaining privacy and informality in their work with helpers, while others provide training or payment to helpers, which serves to explicitly define a set of role expectations. At what point does formalization occur and for what purpose is it incompatible?

Role of Helping Networks

Helping networks are not a simple or homogeneous social collectivity but vary widely in purpose, membership and structure. In situations where there are internal value conflicts among members of a network, where norms of reciprocity may hinder certain kinds of helping or where the network is characterized by cliques that serve to exclude people from membership, the role of a helping network in working with an agency may become ambiguous. How do these factors influence who an agency staff can and cannot serve if they are to establish links with a helping network? The agency should strive to overcome these barriers through information, training and contact with the various factions. Roles and task may be assigned to handle the conflicts in a culturally sensitive manner.

Relating the Formal to the Informal

Interaction between an agency and helping networks depends upon the nature of exchange and the compatibility of objectives and values to which such exchange is directed. What happens when there is a difference in objectives? An agency concerned with promoting self-sufficiency and a network concerned with obtaining tangible resources may encounter difficulties in coming to a common basis for exchange. One may want to be non-directive while the other may be asking for direction. Further, some agencies see themselves as phasing out their work with a network while others are concerned with developing an ongoing relationship. What kinds of helping networks or what types of informal helping are suited to these contrasting objectives? Agencies should provide advocacy to obtain resources for basic human needs and provide support for self sufficiency in areas where the client expressed needs indicate such. There should be a dual focus. Finally, in working with neighborhoods or helping networks with strong norms deriving from tradition or culture, to what extent must agency staff adapt themselves to these norms if they are effectively to relate to informal helpers? What is gained and lost in the process of adaptation? There must be an understanding and appreciation of the sensitivity, and incorporation of these norms in their service delivery process.

The various approaches researched on the ten programs illustrate how matters of context, purpose, interaction and role definition may be considered and decided upon in practice. Yet, the approaches presented offer answers that must be refined by further experience with alternative strategies of development in different settings. There are many reasons for professionals to begin working with informal helping networks and there is a developing body of experience to suggest ways in which this might be done.

Summary

Beginning with the Social Security Act of 1935, social programs and legislation have been increasingly aimed at defining and meeting the needs of the elderly. While much of the thrust has been generated in the last two decades and is attributable, in part, to the simple fact that the older portion of the United States population is growing at an unprecedented rate, it would be misleading to suggest that the growth of legislation and social programs for the aged is a simple function of a higher proportion of elderly in the population.

Kamerman (1976) suggested that the mobilization of an organized constituency of older Americans was precipitated not only by a numerical increase of the elderly but also influenced by the Civil Rights Movement in the 60s, which stressed minority rights. It was only in the 60s that the aged emerged for the first time as a powerful political interest group. There is little question that the aged—representing 10 percent of the total population and 17 percent of eligible voters—are a powerful and articulate interest group.

As a consequence of the bulge at the older portion of the population and their potentioal political potency, the demand for concomitant change in the service institutions designed for the elderly is apparent. Because the elderly are a widely heterogenous group with needs which become more specialized and diverse as impairments and dysfunctions compound, it has been demanded that any system developed or expanded must incorporate a variety of services to meet such diversity (Hendricks, 1977). Additionally the demand has been made for service to be more efficient and effective by having some degree of adaptability and accessibility to respond quickly to rising needs and new situations. Furthermore, services must be integrated in mutually supporting ways with other relevant service systems and components. Demands have been made to draw from all possible human resources, including professional and non professional staff and volunteers, as well as others in the community who are not professionally involved in providing services (Tobin, 1976).

It is suggested here that because of the political activity initiated primarily by the aged as an interest group, elected policy makers have become more attentive to the "plight" of the elderly and have responded by increasing spending for the aged in federal, state and local governments; the likelihood is great that more will be spent in the future. These programs are complex, both in terms of historic ignorance and opposition to "welfare programs"; therefore it is imperative not only that the needs of older persons be analyzed and evaluated more vigorously than in the past, but also that the sources of their deprivation be discovered and publicized.

Our recent history points out that expansions in social programs alone will not resolve some of the underlying issues that precipitated the development of specific social legislation. A retrospective analysis of the War On Poverty points to possible reasons for the demise of economic opportunity programs and may well serve as a caution to what appears to be inevitable policy and program expansions related to the elderly in the near future.

Depending largely upon the different viewpoints and preferences of those assessing the War on Poverty programs generally, and Comunity Action Programs specifically, it was assumed that the nature of major provisions would take one of the three forms: 1) an instrument to coordinate the planning and delivery of services; 2) an expansion in the level of services made available to the poor; or 3) an increase in decision-making powers of the poor to formulate and administer their own local programs (Gilbert and Specht, 1974).

Because legislation had been broadly defined to encompass all of these provisions two important elements were left unclear. First was the order and priority to be given to these provisions; that various provisions were inconsistent with one another was largely overlooked. Second, there was little probing of the substance of these various social provisions. For example, how much power and influence was concealed in the concept "maximum feasible participation"? Did "Participation" mean that the poor were to be advisors or have a controlling vote? More significantly, what types of services did the poor *need* and *want*? "Serious consideration of these choices would have delayed passage of the legislation. Instead it sailed through Congress on the ethereal plane of abstraction" (Gilbert and Specht, 1974:94). When, however, it finally came down to implementation and efforts were made to specify and operationalize phrases such as "maximum feasible participation," the programs provoked a sense of betrayal and encountered heavy resistance.

It is important to note that the "political lives" of elected public officials in the United States are constantly under scrutiny by various constituencies. The public sector, on the other hand, has developed some degree of confidence in their elected representatives. If this confidence is misplaced, the officials lose credibility and may suffer at the polls. As a result of this checks-and-balance system, policy development and program production are more a reflection of constituents' desires than a clear grasp of the theoretical and tentative quality of policy objectives. The concern here is to strike a balance between policy decisions that have become an accepted way to "continue a political life" and those which attempt to facilitate the development and use of services for those purported to be served.

One way to facilitate the development and use of services for older Americans is to be sensitive to their needs. An approach to understanding the needs of the elderly is to be aware of the aging process in the latter half of the life cycle. It is important, for example, to consider both the common crisis encountered by the aged and the traditional systematic supports available. This approach tends to be global in its application and seems to have as one of its advantages an accurate picture of the elderly as a single aged group.

It is true that an effective delivery of social services to older Americans involves, at the very least, policy decisions regarding who is to be the recipient of services, what is to be delivered, and how it is to be organized (Tobin, 1977). Therefore, it appears that before an effective service delivery system can be created, issues of who, what and how must be resolved. In defining the "who," it is important to consider the relative advantages of serving all elderly or only the particularly vulnerable. Inasmuch as the all-elderly population does include the vulnerable, one cannot overlook the latter subgroup when discussing the former; yet, it can be shown that the effect of underemphasizing the vulnerable is to exclude them. Even though the elderly are defined as a single population at risk, for some subgroups the risk is greater than it is for others.

Minorities are concerned that erroneous sterotypes emerge from the practice of categorizing all aged people into a single entity. Their concern stems from the fact that, although research of the elderly has proliferated, along with the growing awareness of the plight of old people, the bulk of social science research has been directed toward the Anglo portion of the population. Whether the social stigma attached to being old or the elderly's own affinity for people for their age provides sufficient grounds for a subculture to evolve to the point where older people became a voting bloc is a question that cannot presently be answered in spite of my previous assessment of the growing militancy among old people. We are concerned that assumptions such as the "subculture" theory may well be untrue but that expensive delivery systems will be designed before explorations for possible differences can be discerned.

For a truly effective service delivery system for the black elderly it may be that common types of service will need to be very differently designed. It is unfortunate that the emphasis on formal social welfare and health care delivery systems has been limited to fitting the individual requirements of older Americans (generally) and ethnic minorities (specifically) to the system, rather than making the system flexible enough to respond to their specific requirements and needs. If social planners are to design programs that effectively meet the needs of black aged, they must become cognizant of existing arrangements utilized by minorities in order that they might integrate a well-developed system that is efficient, effective and humane.

References

Collins, A., & Pancoast, D. *Natural helping networks*. Washington, D.C.: National Association of Social Workers, 1976.

Estes, C. *The aging enterprise*. San Francisco: Jose-Bass Publishers, 1979.

Faulkner, A. The black aged as good neighbors: An experiment in volunteer service. Address delivered at the Scientific Meeting of the Gerontological Society, Miami Beach, Florida, 1973.

Froland, C., Chapman, N., Kimboko, D., & Pancoast, D. *Linking helping networks with human services*. Regional Research Institute, Portland State University, January, 1979.

Future directions for aging policy a human service model. A report by the Subcommittee on Human Services of the Select Committee on Aging U.S. House of Representatives 96th Congress, 2nd Session Committee publicaiton No. 96-226, U.S. Government Printing Office, Washington, D.C.: May, 1980.

Gilbert, N. & Specht, H. *Dimension of social welfare policy*. New Jersey: Prentice-Hall, Inc., 1974.

Hendricks, J., & Hendricks, D. *Aging in mass society: Myths and realities.* Cambridge, Massachusetts: Winthrop Publishers, Inc., 1977.

Kamerman, S.B., & Kahn, A.J. *Social services in the United States: Policies and programs.* Philadelphia: Temple University Press, 1976.

National Commission on Neighborhoods. *People building neighborhoods.* Final Report to the President and the Congress of the United States. Washington, D.C.: U.S. Government Printing Office, March 19, 1979.

President's Commission on Mental Health, *Report of the task panel on community support systems.* Washington, D.C.: U.S. Government Printing Office, 1978.

Tobin, S., Davidson, S. & Sack, A. *Effective social services for older Americans.* Detroit, Michigan: Institute of Gerontology, Wayne State University, 1976.

Bill Chin, Coordinator
Multi-Service Center Project
San Jose, CA

THE MULTIPURPOSE SENIOR CENTER:
ACCESS TO COMPREHENSIVE AND COORDINATED SERVICES
FOR THE MINORITY ELDERLY?

Introduction

Human service professionals, and lay people interested in human services, over the years have collected a handful of cherished program concepts. Every decade or so, one or more of these is taken off the shelf, dusted off, a few updated drippings are added and it is offered as a panacea for whatever ails you. The program concepts are so logical and attractive that no amount of past failures can discourage us from giving it just one more try.

One of these concepts is that of service delivery through a multiservice center, community service center, focal point, multipurpose senior center, and the like. By whatever name, the centers were developed for basically the same purpose—to improve the service delivery system through a single entry point to comprehensive and coordinated services. The reason the idea keeps coming back is, of course, a sad commentary on the way human services have been and continue to be delivered.

Within the last quarter century a proliferation of new programs have been started. This has led to new organizations of the federal, state and local levels, and in the private sector. These new programs are serving an increasing number of people, but are also serving identified special needs of various segments of the population.

Services are delivered in a fragmented, uncoordinated way, which means that each service program is adminsitered by a different division of an agency or by different agencies. These agencies are separated from one another by geography, by different authorizing legislation and operational guidelines, by conflicting eligibility criteria, and by different goals and objectives to be achieved with the services to be provided. Often these services are not even aware of the existence of others, or that they may be serving the same individual or family. As a result, a person with multiple needs spends a large amount of time going from one provider to the other as his/her needs are compartmentalized and fitted into the neat little boxes of the narrow restirctions of each program. We must begin to understand that we need to view the person as a "whole person" whose multiple needs have a direct relationship to one another.

Older Americans Act

The major focus of the Older Americans Act charges state and local communities to develop comprehensive and coordinated systems for service delivery to older persons. Two programs eligible for funding under the act to assist in the development of comprehensive and coordinated service delivery systems are multipurpose senior centers and community focal points. Multipurpose senior centers has been defined in the act as a "community facility for the organization and provision of a broad spectrum of services for older persons." The 1978 ammendments require the area agency on aging to "designate, where feasible, a focal point for comprehensive service delivery in each community to encourage the maximum collocation and coordination of services for older individuals, and to give special consideration to designating multipurpose senior centers as such focal points. In addition, the 1978 amendments authorize, for the first time, provisions for funding the ascquisition, alteration, renovation, and construction of new facilities to serve as multipurpose senior centers, and authorize the secretary of health and human services to insure any mortgage, under certain conditions, which covers a multipurpose senior center. As a consequence of these provisions, it is quite clear that the intent of Congress is that the multipurpose senior centers will play a very large part in meeting the charge to develop comprehensive and coordinated services to older people.

Characteristics of a Multipurpose Senior Center

Morris Cohen, who was special assistant to the director, Office of State and Community Programs, Administration on Aging, talks about the following in a 1977 paper:

Community Visibility

The designation of a specific facility for older persons is certainly one indication of a community's concern for its older citizens. An attractive building designed to provide the necessary space for programs and services can actually change out-dated community attitudes toward older people.

Central Location for Services

A center can provide accessibility to essential services in one distinct location, or make them available through linkages developed by the center. The central location can also provide the base for a concerted outreach component.

Focal Point

The center provides older people a focal point for their concerns and interests that is generally not available in any other type of facility.

Bridge to the Community

The center is a part of the community. To participate in center activities is to participate in the life of the community. The center, through its various programs, helps older persons to feel that they can and should continue to contribute to their community, and that they are wanted and valued members of that community.

Program Elements

Broadly speaking, the program element includes all the activities and services that occur in the center. Multipurpose senior centers, in collaboration with other agencies and organizations, can provide all or some of the following services.

Recreation—The opportunity to participate either alone, or in groups, in creative efforts or in programs which encourage socialization: arts and crafts; nature, science and outdoors; drama; music; physical activity; excursions.

Education—Services meant to inform, enlighten, satisy curiosity or encourage action: health education; adult education; college classes; crime prevention; financial management.

Information and Referral—A central detailed reference service about community services and resources; formalized referral services not available at the center; and follow-up to determine linkage.

Case Management—To provide individualized assessment of the person's situation and needs; to identify services to meet those needs and coordinate the delivery of those services; to provide follow-up and insure that services are provided in an appropriate manner; and to identify and correct problems within the service system that prevent the person from receiving needed services.

Specific Direct Services may include—health; income maintenance; mental health; protective services; nutrition; in-home supportive services; day care; adult day health; housing; transportation; employment; legal; escort; telephone assurance; friendly visiting; home health aid; volunteer; others.

It is obvious that no one center can coordinate or house the above laundry list of services. Aggrements and arrangements, preferably formalized, should be developed with both in-center and out-of-center services to ensure that they are available to the elderly participant of the center. The services to be located at the center should be determined as a part of the planning process which should include an assessment of the community's needs and a determination of the most appropriate service mix.

Past Experiences in Coordination

The last section discussed briefly the potential for a multipurpose senior center. The focus was primarily on comprehensiveness of services. A brief review of the findings of two surveys on services integration and case coordination projects may assist us in planning multipurpose senior centers. The first, by Gans and Horton (Integration of Human Services—The state and Local Level, 1975), talks about various factors which facilitate and inhibit services integration. They define social services integration as "the linking together by various means of two or more service providers to allow treatment of an individual's or family's needs in a more coordinated and comprehensive manner."

1. *The Environment*

   The sociopolitical environment in which the project functions is an important factor, both positive and negative. Support from government, community and public and private funding sources, in terms of the need for service delivery changes in general and by means of the project in particular, often enhances integrative efforts, while opposition exerts an important negative influence.

2. *Project Objectives and Priorities*

   A critical inhibitor to service integration is the lack of attention given to integrative efforts by the projects, most salient being an emphasis on service delivery responsibility and internal operations, and a definition of project objectives that do not recognize the establishment of integrative linkages as a central part of the project mission.

3. *Project Director*

   The study provides support for the "great man/woman" theory that the personality of the project director is one of the most important factors in services integration.

4. *Project Staff*

   A critical facilitator or service integration is the existence of a capable staff whose mission is the coordination of providers and not service delivery.

5. *Service Providers' Objectives and Attitudes*

   The attitudes of service providers have great impact on service integration efforts. Where providers want to retain absolute control of funds, functions, and internal procedures, and where they vie for control of the delivery system, services integration is impeded. If, in addition, providers have their own power and influence with funding sources, attempts to overcome attidinal obstacles are particularly hindered.

6. *Grant Administration Policies and Procedures*

   Services integration is facilitated to the extent the project integrator has control over service providers' access to funding. This control enables the integrator to require provider participation in linkages as a prerequisite to receiving funding. Open-ended funding of the project facilitates services integration. In-such a project, the integrator could hold out hte promise of continuing and on going funding. Unclear guidelines and funding delays causes projects and staff to turn their attention to survival rather than coordination.

The second survey, by the University of Southern California's Andrus Gerontology Center in 1977 resulted in a list of "lessons" on case coordination:

1. No one program model suits all communities.

2. The Agency which coordinates other agencies should not operate direct services.

3. Coordination is very expensive, as well as difficult. Do not try to coordinate too many agencies at once.

4. Public/voluntary agency funding contracts can work, but successful coordination requires moderate stress.

5. Community and consumer involvement is difficult, takes time and is a two-edged sword. Different degrees of community control are indicated for different kinds of objectives.

6. Collocation does not equal coordination. Unification of different services under one administration does not guarantee coordination.

7. Authority helps, but does not guarantee coordination. Cooperative models rarely succeed.

8. Accountability mechanisms are hellish to install and maintain, but can be productive in time.

9. A coordination system should be evolutionary and cumulative.

10. The potential efficiency and effectiveness of a coordination system cannot be evaluated during the first and second years. (This does not preclude performance monitoring and documenting the experience and rate of progress.)

11. The leader of a coordination project must be a super being with optimum political skills, administrative competence, missionary fervor and familiarity with the entire range of professional interventions and management techniques. In addition, the leader must, during the early phase of the project, be primarily process-oriented and in lager phases, be primarily task-oriented.

12. At all levels of coordination, it is critical that there be frequent and genuine interpersonal contact between representatives of agencies who are essential to the program success.

Multipurpose Senior Center Impact on the Minority Elderly

Having discussed some of the advantages and problems of multipurpose senior centers, the issue left to us is whether a center will improve on the delivery of services needed by the minority elderly. There is little disagreement that the present fragmented, uncoordinated and unresponsive service delivery system has not served the minority elderly well, and must abe changed and improved. Some of the issues that need to be considered include:

1. To ensure that the minority community and its elderly in particular, have a voice in determining whether such a center is desired in the community, or whether there are other alternatives to ensure improved access to a comprehensive and coordinated system.

2. To ensure that the minority community be involved in the planning, development, implementation and administration of the center, including: location; service mix; bilingual and/or bicultural staffing; employment opportunities for community residents, particularly the elderly; auspices under which the center will operate; formal and informal mechanism that will be available for continuing input.

3. Strategies which will ensure that the minority communities receive a fair share of funds allocated for such centers or alternative methods of accessing the minority elderly to comprehensive and coordinated services.

References

Cohen, M. *The multipurpose senior center: Characteristics, purpose, and elements.* Administration on Aging, Office of Human Services, U.S. Dept. of Health and Human Services, 1977.

Miller, J. *Multipurpose senior project: A concept paper.* Health and Welfare Agency, State of California, 1978.

Gans, S.P., & Horton, G.T. *Integration of human services: The state and municipal levels.* New York, Praeger Publishers, 1975.

Steinberg, R.M. *Case coordination: Lessons from the past for future program models.* Unpublished paper, University of Southern California, 1978.

Evalyn G. Greb, M.S.W.
Director
Multipurpose Senior Service Project
San Diego, California

CALIFORNIA MULTIPURPOSE SENIOR SERVICES PROJECT

In California at present, thirteen separate state and federal agencies administer around thirty different categorical service programs for the elderly, yet no structure exists to insure that these resources are applied in a consistent and comprehensive manner to effectively address the needs of the elderly. Many of the elderly persons who will require supportive services will not be able to obtain those services with their own resources when you consider that approximately 25 percent of the total population over age 65 have incomes below the near-poverty level. Each categorical program has its own eligibility levels, needs, assessment criteria, processes and service coverage limitations. In the face of rapidly escalating costs for publicaly subsidized services for the elderly, California must improve its service systems. The fragmentation of the current non-systems of services results in a number of substantial problems. Most notably, it is inequitable, ineffective and inefficient, and results in inappropriate incentives for improving the health and independence of moderately impaired or frail elderly persons.

The current system of services treats frail elderly persons inequitably in that persons in similar health and socioeconomic circumstances, and with similar supportive services needs, may receive entirely different services with very different results. Services programs and attendant outcomes are more a function of the point of entry into the service system than of the circumstances and needs of the person. For example, one elderly person with a health problem which substantially restricts his mobility may go to his doctor for help. The physician may decide that placement in a skilled nuring facility is most appropriate to meet his patient's needs. The placement is made and the outcome of the services is the general physical and mental deterioration which so often characterizes nursing-home placement.

Another elderly person, one with an identical or similar health problem and in a similar socio-economic status, may seek help from a social worker at the county welfare department. The social worker may mobilize in-home supportive service resources, augmented with periodic visits from a public health nurse or an adult day health program. The services are provided and the outcomes are improved health status and increased independence. This example serves to illustrate the point: the nature and extent of supportive services now provided to elderly persons are determined more by the type of system the person contacts for help than by a comprehensive and critical assessment of the person's needs. This lack of a centralized authority and standards for needs assessment and attendant resource allocation is the direct and immediate cause of the inequity described above.

The current system is not effective in that the apparent purpose for public subsidy of the various categorical programs serving the elderly is to improve the quality of their lives; that is, to maintain their health and wellbeing at a level where they can continue to function independently within and productively interact with society in general. The current system of service is not meeting this goal. Rather than fostering independence, the system appears to generate further dependence on the system. In fact, thousands of patients are admitted to skilled nursing facilities annually. At any one time, it is estimated that from 80 to 90 percent of the patients in a skilled nursing facility will stay there for two to three years. Their prognosis for recovery, rehabilitation and eventual return home is poor.

Until relatively recently, long- term institutional care represented the only publicly-funded alternative for dealing with the needs of the elderly. Even now, with alternative services funded through programs such as those provided through the Older Americans Act and Title XX, the service system is not effectively meeting the goal described above. The bulk of public funds for supportive services for the elderly still subsidize long-term institutional care, and the available alternatives are applied sporadically within the constraints of the categorical programs.

The current system is inefficient. As more and more financial resources are allocated to the system of social and health services to elderly Californians, dependence on those service programs is increased, generating additional demand for resources. The idiosyncracies of the categorical program requirements contribute to this inefeciency. Each individual program attempting to serve the elderly is confined to doing that which is specifically provided by law and regulation; it cannot do that which a comprehensive assessment of the client's needs would indicate should be done. Often, necessary complimentary services are not available. For example. in an individual case, homemaker services may need to be complimented with physical therapy to meet the case goal of fostering client independence. Since these two necessary services are funded via two separate categorical programs, there is no coordinated structure to assure that both services are provided within the context of a comprehensive program to improve daily functioning and independence; and typically, they are not. Either one provided independent of the other will not meet the established goal, even though substantial resources may have been expended. Rather, it is likely that the result will be continued, or even increased requirements for supportive services from the system.

Other inefficiencies result from categorical funding structures. For example, Title XX, which supports in-home supportive services, has a closed-end budget; Title XIX, which supports Medi-Cal, does not. When Title XX funds are exhausted, the most available alternative is to place the client in a nursing home—generally at a higher cost to the public, and with less beneficial results.

The current system fosters inappropriate incentives. Actually, this theme runs through the discussion of the problems mentioned above; inequity, ineffectiveness and inefficiency; but its importance deserves further consideration here. As mentioned above, the expressed goal of publicly-funded service programs for the elderly is to improve their level of functioning and reduce their reliance on those service programs. Currently, the system of incentives is reversed: the longer a patient stays in a skilled nursing facility, the more money the facility makes; the larger the county's in-home supportive service caseload is, the more federal and state dollars flow into the county. Such incentives are inevitable within the state's economic system, but to equitably, effectively, and efficiently meet the needs of California's elderly, they must be at least counter-balanced with the judgment of authoritative experts dedicated to improving the independence of capable frail elderly.

It was based on this information that Assemblyman Leo T. McCarthy sponsored and Governor Jerry Brown signed Assembly Bill 998 in 1978, which included the authority to establish a demonstration effort entitled the Multipurpose Senior Services Project (MSSP). The California Legislative intent established the purpose of the MSSP to develop information about effective methods:

a) to prevent premature disengagement of older persons from their indigenous communities and subsequent dommitment to institutions.

b) to provide optimum accessibility of various important community social and health resources available to assist active older persons to maintain independent living.

c) to provide that the "at risk" moderately impaired or frail older person who has the capacity to remain in an independent living situation has access to the appropriate services.

d) to provide the most efficient and effective use of public funds in the delivery of these social and health services.

e) to coordinate, integrate, and link these social and health services including county social services by removing obstacles which impede or limit improvements in delivery of these services.

f) to allow the State substantial flexibilty in organizing or administering the delivery of social and health services to its senior citizens.

Project Objectives

The Project has been designed as a research effort. In developing the design the MSSP has defined the above objectives in such a way as to allow some comparison to be made among the eight project sites, and to allow comparison between MSSP participants and non-MSSP participants.

These comparative objectives are:

1. to reduce the clients' number of days as a hospital patient;

2.   to reduce the clients' number of days as a skilled nursing facility patient;

3.   to reduce the total public expenditures on social and health services for clients and;

4.   to improve or maintain the clients' functional abilities, both physical and psychological.

These objectives are within the guidelines in the State Plan on Aging for Fiscal Year 1981-1983 by the California Department on Aging.   Under 4C.2 in that document the department has established as one of their goals, system development to insure/design a system which is responsive to older persons with multiple economic and social needs, including cultural and physical needs in non-institutionalized as well as institutionalized settings by establishing a continuity of service provision across services and assisting AAAs in strengthening relationships among local entities to provide an array of services to older persons.
These objectives are to:

> Ensure that older persons who require assistance to carry out activities of daily living due to physical, mental, economic and/or social impairments to their functional capacity have full and prompt access to a system of services designed to provide the most approproate level of care in the least restrictive setting possible.

Objectives have been outlined legislatively to be used in measuring the MSSP's effectiveness and efficiency overall.   There is one basic *operational* question, which is: Recognizing the feasible alternatives within the existing social and health services system, what iptions are most likely to make the largest contribuiton to improving the system's overall performance?   Towards this end, the following MSSP operations objectives are:

1.   to estimate the effective services;

2.   to estimate more effective service mixes;

3.   to estimate more effective service mixes;

4.   to estimate the optimal expenditures on client care while reducing skilled nursing facility care and hospital patient days and;

5.   to estimate the optimal expenditure on client care while

6.   improving or maintianing client's physical and psychological functional gains.

Project Sites

The design of the Multipurpose Senior Services Project demonstration calls for eight sites chosen from around the state to represent a variety of service delivery models, geographic areas, and client backgrounds. The agencies administering these sites are:

1. City of Oakland
2. County of Santa Cruz
3. East Los Angeles Health Task Force, Inc.
4. Jewish Family Service of Los Angeles
5. Senior Care Action Network, Long Beach
6. San Francisco (Mt. Zion Consortium)
7. San Diego County Area Agency on Aging
8. The Greater Ukiah Senior Citizens Center

These sites will provide services for a total client population of 1900 persons. A comparison group of approximately 1300 will be followed to provide information on the impact and cost of services provided through the traditional health/social service delivery system.

The site staff at each Multipurpose Senior Services Project are not involved in the control group process, but a separate entity has been hired to assess the 2300 control group participants.

Eligibility

In the research design of the MSSP, much care was given to avoiding what ic called "creaming" of the seniors in the community who already are active and have access to other community services. Because of that, eligiblity was established within four phase-in groups in the project. All eligibility criteria limit participation in the program to those persons 65 years of age and older who are currently eligible for Medi-Cal and who meet the target criteria within one of the four phases.

Phase I included 25 percent of the total caseload, and individuals were picked up through:

1) outreach efforts conducted by sites.

2) by applying the activities of daily living index to define the potential clients' functional level then obtaining roughly equal numbers of clients in three functional levels (low, medium, and high).

In Phase II, the hospital phase, sites established a working relationship with hospitals in the catchment area in order to identify and secure 40 percent of their clients. This was one of the two random sample phases, and 111 clients who were potentially eligible by virtue of being 65, residing within the catchment area, being on Medi-Cal were approached to participate in the project. Three attempts were made to complete the interview with each of these potential clients before rejecting the patient as a possible MSSP client.

In Phase III, the skilled nursing facility phase, which was the second of the two random sample phases, the sites were required to establish a working relationship with nursing homes in the area with the assistance of the Medi-Cal field office. The actual procedure consisted of collecting names off the treatment authorization request for skilled nursing facility placements at the Medi-Cal field office. The site staff then went down the list without discrimination and interviewed individuals and their treating physicians to secure participation in the program. Once again three attempts were made to complete the interview before rejecting the patient as a possible MSSP client. Ten percent of total site caseload was picked up in this manner.

Phase IV, the second community phase, also targeted 25 percent of the client caseload. The criteria as mandated by the state MSSP for this particular phase was as follows:

1.   if a person was hospitalized at the time

2.   if a person has been hospitalized within the last six months;

3.   if a person score mild, or moderately severe on the MSQ;

4.   if a person qualify according to the social resources rating scale and

5.   if a person fell into a low ADL status.

The clients above were all taken in and each site had its full caseload compliment by February 28, 1981. Persons who met the project eligibility criteria and who were accepted as clients were thoroughly assessed in terms of their social, functional, physical, and psychological status. A nurse practitioner and social worker team have primary responsibility for obtaining the assessment information. The client's existing levels of service utilization and informal support are determined at the time of intake.

The core of the MSSP approach is the role of the senior services counselor as case manager. The functions of a case manager include the full continuum of client care: 1) to develop a relationship at a level to insure an individualized, holistic assessment of the client's situation and functional limitations in order to establish and clarify needs; 2) to identify services and informal supports to meet those needs and coordinate the delivery of such services; 3) to monitor and evaluate the delivery of services to insure ongoing appropriateness, effectiveness and client satisfaction; 4) to deal as broker, monitor, problem-solver within policy and service provider systems. These functions cover eight major categories of client-oriented services:

1.   *outreach* to enrol the frail/homebound;

2.   sophisticated, formalized *assessment* of client to include: elibility, demographic information, "activities of daily living" status (Katz's scale), mental status, personal and family history, evaluation of family and/or informal support systems, current service utilization, medical and health history and status, release authorization for information from doctors.

3.   *treatment plan* which includes ordering services for clients and

monitoring their quality and effectiveness, working with family and support systems to maximize plan.

4. *review assessment* monthly (more frequently in the face of trauma or an unusual event; i.e., hospitalization).

5. *reassesses quarterly* to adjust level of care to changing need in fragile (all) client load.

6. *maintain client records* to reflect all of the above.

7. *contract* with all community groups/services/agencies/ facilities whether formally or informally to provide services needed by clients.

8. *keeps overview* of gaps, grievances, problems (to include legislative and policy as well as client-oriented).

Service Waivers

In order to have maximum flexibility to provide the services currently not available to elderly clients or to be able to provide services through single, coordinating agency, the MSSP requested waivers from some existing Social Security Title XIX (Medicaid or "Medi-Cal") regulations. The principal waivers requested added several services to those that may be provided using Title XIX funds. Those new services are:

1. *Adult Social Day Care* which provides day time social, recreational and nutriotional services; housing which provides assistance in locating housing, moving expenses and minor home repairs.

2. *In-Home Supportive Services* which provides basic household and personal care services;

3. *Legal Services* which provides assistance in circumstances such as eviction, public assistance difficulties, property losses, involuntary commitments and consumer problems;

4. *Respite Care* which provides supervision to persons while the usual person providing care pursues other activities;

5. *Non-Medical Transportation* which provides persons with access to the community;

6. *Meal Services* which provides meals to persons who cannot prepare their own meals or who need congregate meals for socialization purposes.

7. *Protective Services* which provides protection to people who are being abused, neglected or exploited;

8.   *Special Communication* which provides devices to assist physically impaired persons to communicate routinely or in the event of an emergency;

9.   *Preventive Health Care* which provides physical examinations to prevent the onset, occurence or effect of potentially debilitating illnesses; and

10. *Special Services* defined by client need.

Information System

Of major research impact is that all client information and care data will be contained within the project information system. This system utilizes an on-line, interactive computer. Now in early states, care plan data will be limited to information on available services providers and projections of care plan costs. As the caseload information is increased, information is provided to the case manager on the "general practice" of service prescription for clients with characteristics similar to his/her own. This information will be developed utilizing data from all eight sites.

Once the data base has been further built up, after six to nine months of operations, algorithms will be constructed based on what services and what levels of services were awarded for different kinds of clients' characteristics and problems. Upon inquiry by the case managers, these algorithms will produce ranges of services awarded, specific to clients' characteristics. The ranges are meant to be guidelines for the counselors and assessment team when they deal with individual clients. As the demonstration continues, outcome data, in terms of reduced hospital and skilled nursing days, will refine the algorithms so that the counselor and assessment team will have the best information on "what works" when they make decisions about individual clients.

In addition to lending assistance to the services staff, the management information system is able to assist scheduling of clients and administrative functions, e.g., accounting, budgeting and billing related to project management. The management information system also has the capability to carry out the statistical analysis related to the evaluation and research components of the Project.

Evaluation

The general evaluation plan calls for the formation of comparison groups which are made up of randomly-selected Medi-Cal recipients, 65 years of age and over, who meet the MSSP eligibility criteria. These individuals are identified through the Medi-Cal master file, then interviewed to determine whether they meet the MSSP eligibility criteria. These individuals are identified through the Medi-Cal master file, then interviewed to determine whether they meet MSSP eligibility criteria and asked if they agree to participate. Assessment/reassessment of this group is conducted in the same manner as that used for the MSSP clients. However, the more comprehensive MSSP services program will not be available to them.

The evaluation plan tests the objectives of the demonstration in the form of null hypotheses to determine whether the MSSP demonstration is successful and to what degree, as compared with the results of the comparison groups. The evaluation plan estimates which services and services mixes are more effective for which participants in terms of the objectives stated earlier. Clients will receive services (as scheduled now) through November 1982, and statistical analysis will be available sometime after that.

Funding

The distinctive feature of the MSSP project is that it pools a number of funding sources to carry out the project. This means that portions of the state general fund, federal Medicaid (Title XIX of the Social Security Act referred to as Medi-Cal in California), Title XX of the Social Security Act (state mandated social services), and the Older Americans Act (Title IIIB) have been pooled into a single funding source for services normally funded through separate categorical programs. Approximately \$43.8 million will be available from these sources over the live of the project, the major portion will be federal and state funding through the Medi-Cal Progra.

It is estimated that the prospective clients are already utilizing ten million dollars of governmentally-supported servces. This results in a net increase of approximately 33.8 million dollars. This increase will be chared 50-50 by the federal and state governments. Non-research related costs average approximately 704 dollars per client per month. This is estimated to be 70 percent the monthly cost were the client to be institutionalized.

Assessment Tool

The one function of the MSSP assessment insturment is to generate infromation, which will be used for determining client eligibility, providing appropriate services to these clients, and for meeting the research needs of the project. The research needs consist of being able to determine the functional status of participants and its change over time, the patterns of service utilization, and the costs of services provided. The local MSSP staff considers this tool to be a unique feature of the project which allows for more complete and holistic treatment planning.

There are five sections of the assessment tool. The first includes *assessment information* which is basic client data. The second or the *MSSP Inquiry Form* is the basic tool for determining target group eligibility. Section three, the *Functional Assessment*, consists of the following components:

1. Demographic Information
2. Activities of Daily Living
3. Mental Status Questions
4. Instrumental Activities of Daily Living
5. Life Satisfaction
6. Family (Children, Brothers, and Sisters)
7. Evaluation of Family and Informal Support System
8. Current Services Utilization Profile
9. Medical Information
10. Summary Interviewer's Judgment

The final section of the instrument is the client care plan. This section is done in case conference with the supervising case manager the case manager, case aid and the nurse practitioner for the client present and all adding to the discussion around the plan that will enhance the wellbeing, increase the self-sufficiency and dependency of the client.

In summary, let me state that the Multipurpose Senior Services Project is looking at the expanded use and documentation of the natural support systems providing personal and social support services to the frail elderly at risk of institutionalization. The need to promote, support and strengthen the natural support system is an even greater need within the framework of the minority elderly. Though it is in contrast to the present service delivery system which has emphasized formal networks, an adequate service system in the future must address the personal and social needs of the minority elderly by recognizing the unique, historical, and cultural experiences of this population. Poor service utilization is not only caused by these differenced, but also by the prejudices and biases of those who legislate, authorize and deal with the minorities, and who must now look closely at philosophical, educational, physiological and environmental differences. Conscious considerations of these differences are mandatory in planning for future systems.

According to one of the case managers at the MSSP who is himself of Hispanic origin, the MSSP is an idealistic program for minorities. Because of language and cultural differences, minorities seem not to participate fully in programs and services available in the community. He believes that some of the specific reasons for this are:

1. lack of coordinated transportation which is accessible to non English-speaking minority groups;

2. minority seniors are not informed about agencies and services in the community and therefore have no access to same;

3. many agencies and programs in the community are not staffed with bilingual and cultural staff and are not 100 percent sensitive to minority needs;

4. minority group elderly are the ones most likely to be referred from one agency to another, with no service provision due to lack of understanding and no follow-up;

5. minority seniors benefit greatly from the coordinated services and team approach of the MSSP, but are especially assisted by the advocacy and follow-up services.

6. all seniors in general, but especially the minorities, are extremely afraid to go into an institution because of the staff, the difference of foods, atmsophere, etc.

Within the MSSP, the nurse practitioner can provide access to health services as well as provide education through the Hispanic case manager. Theoretically, if every senior center in every town in every state had a cultural representative of each of the large minority groups, these minorities would be represented and would have access to all services available in the community with the interpretation and cultural bridging provided by the case manager. To date, the San Diego MSSP has the following breakdown of minority clients: black 24, Hispanic 18, Pan Asian 4, Other 6.

Turning to the executive summary of the 7th National Institute on Minority Aging that was held in San Diego last February, the minority population aged 65 years and over has a growth pattern at almost twice the rate of the total population. It is anticipated that the figure will reach 5.1 million by the year 2000, as compared to 2.9 million in 1978. These demographic projections underscore the critical need for culturally compatible research in training, planning and implementing future programs for minority elders. Hopefully, one of the MSSP research findings will be to provide quantitative and qualitative aspects of minority needs in order to establish meaningful policy and service programs to meet future needs for the community services.

Vladimir Einisman, M.D.
The Gerontology Center
Texas Research Institute of Mental Sciences, Houston

LONG-TERM CARE AND THE MINORITY ELDERLY

The major demographic change of the twentieth century is in the number of people reaching age 65. One in six Americans will be 65 years of age or older by the year 2030 (Southern New England Long-Term Care Gerontology Center, 1980). In 1900 the number of individuals 65 years old and over was 3,000,000 or 4 percent of the population. In 1980 this group included more than 23 million people (Bureau of the Census, 1977, reported by the Institute of Medicine).

With respect to the minority elderly, the 1978 census reported that those 55 years and older numbered 5,400,000. Of those, black elderly persons accounted for almost 90 percent, or 3,872,000. The number of Hispanic elderly 55 years old and older was 1,113,000. Among Asians, 275,000 were 55 years old and older, and American Indians accounted for 89,000 people in that age category (Policy Issues Concerning the Elderly Minorities, 1979).

The percentage of those 85 years old and older has doubled since 1900 and is projected to double again in the next 75 years. The segment of the elderly population that will experience the most rapid growth will be the old-old, or those 75 years old and above, nonwhite persons and women of all races (Public Policy and the Frail Elderly, 1978).

Between 1900 and 1975 the number of persons over 74 years has increased ten times (Hanlon, 1975). Those 75 years old and older constitute 38 percent of the total elderly population. In 1975 the 75-79 age group had 1,500,000 men and 2,400,000 women. By the year 2000 the ratio among those aged 75 and older will be 100 men for 190 women.

The prevalence of mental and physical illnesses increases with age. As Administration on Aging statistics indicate, 86 percent of all elderly persons suffer from at least one or more chronic illnesses. The most affected group is again the old-old, those 75 years old and over (Southeastern New England Long-Term Care Gerontology Center, 1980). The incidence of mental illness also increases with age. If we compare the 35 to 54 age group of 100,000 people, the incidence will be 93.0. For the same number in the 65 years old and older group, the incidence is 236.1. Organic brain syndrome is the most common mental disorder in the elderly. It is estimated that 5 percent of the 23,000 people over 65 are severely affected by organic brain syndrome, as are close to 20 percent of those aged 80 and older.

Thirty percent of all the hospitalized psychiatric patients in the country are more than 65 years old. Although the same group has a 14 percent incidence of depression and functional disorders and the incidence of psychiatric illnesses in the elderly is 3.3 times higher than in the general population, only 4 percent are served by community mental health centers. In outpatient clinics the elderly account for only 2 percent of the patients served, and less than 4 percent of older parients seen by private practitioners are 65 years old and older (Butler, 1975). The incidence of chronic diseases (cerebrovascular diseases, arteriosclerotic heart disease, diabetes, hypertension, osteoarthritis, organic brain syndrome, malignant neoplasms, etc.) increases with age, and thus two-thirds to three-fourths of older people have one chronic illness, and 50 percent suffer from two chronic diseases that limit their functional activity and ability to take care of themselves. They have twice as many general hospital stays and stay in the hospital twice as long as younger people (Busse and Pfeiffer, 1973). Simultaneous occurrences of physical and mental disorders are common also (Cheah, 1975). The 75-year-old and older group is the most vulnerable of all to psychological, physical and environmental stressors (Brody, S., 1975). The more vulnerable in this group are the elderly minorities. Because the growing elderly population has an enormous impact on the economy of the nation, providing a continuum of long-term care should be a high priority for policymakers and service providers at the federal, state and local levels.

In 1977, 41.3 billion dollars were spent on personal health care programs for the elderly (Busse and Pfeiffer, 1977), more than a quarter of all economic resources spent on health in the whole nation. Despite this huge flow of funds, lack of planning, coordination, accessibility, and adequacy of services, and underutilization of natural support systems, lack of education and research, the frail elderly remain underserved or abandoned. Less than 50 percent of the disabled older people receive health and social services (Rose et al., 1980). The minority elderly represent an even higher risk group because they experience a higher incidence of mental and physical diseases, socioeconomic deprivation, cultural insensitivity and disintegration of natural support systems, including their own families, Health services are even more inaccessible to them.

The Concept of Long-Term Care and Its Functions

"Long-term care refers to one or more services provided on a sustained basis to enable individuals whose functional capacities are chronically impaired to be maintained at their maximum levels of health and well-being." (E. Brody, 1977).

Although people of all ages need treatment and supportive services on a continuing basis, those 75 years old and older are a target population for long-term care; physical and mental diseases tend to be permanent. The services may be provided in the home (nursing care, friendly visiting, housekeeping assistance, outside the home (day hospital, senior citizens' centers, consumer education) or perhaps services linked to other agencies (periodica health and social assessment, information and referral, transportation, etc.). These services may be provided in a wide variety of settings (Table 1.).

Table 1.

Long-Term Care Continuum of Services

Personal Services

In Home	Outside Home	Access Protection
Personal care	Personal care	Escort
Homemaker	Consumer education	Transportation
Shopping assistance	Day care	Legal aid
Respite care	Day hospital	Consumer education/
Consumer educa-	Counseling	tation
tion/information	Religious institutions	Information and referral
counseling	(church/synagogue)	Insurance assistance
Home maintenance		Income supplement
		Outreach
		Food stamps

Social Services

Friendly visiting	Congregate meals	Information and referral
Escort services	Interest groups/clubs	Protective services
Telephone	Recreation activities	Advocacy
reassurance	Cultural acttivities	
	Volunteer activities	
	Screening/education	
	Counseling	
	Employment opportunities	

Health Services

Nursing care	Emergency care	Periodic assessment
Home-delivered	Nursing care	(health/social)
meals	Congregate meals	
Nutrition/health	Health assessment/	
education	diagnosis and	
Mental health	treatment (physical	
Physical rehabili-	and mental)	
tation	Physical rehabilitation	
Home health	Health education	
	Equipment: appliancces	
	Eye care	
	Dental care	
	Speech and hearing	
	Case management and	
	screening	
	Hospital care, acute/chronic	

Living Arrangements — Residential Services

Own Home	Congregage Housing	Nursing Home Facility
Home of relative	Independent with meals	Skilled nursing care
or friend	Supervision	Intermediate care
Boarding House	Services	
Group home	Nursing care	
Foster family		
care		

Adapted from *Continuum of Care Report*, Office of Medical Programs, Texas Department of Human Resources, July 2, 1979, and from Long-Term Care Gerontology Center, *Delivery of Services Task Force*, March 31, 1980, Texas Research Institute of Mental Sciences.

Special Consideration in Long-Term Care for the Minority Elderly

Health Needs

Health services are not meeting the needs of the minority elderly because of inadequate gerontological research and lack of training of caregivers who see elderly patients. Lack of appropriate prevention by regular physical examinations and education in nutrition, early detection of cancer and hypertension, antismoking and alcohol programs, partly explain the higher incidence of chronic illnesses and shorter lifespan among the elderly minorities (Raya, 1977). Black people have had higher incidence of chronic degenerative diseases (Manton, 1980), hypertension, cerebrovascualar accidents, and cancer (Jackson, 1980).

Obesity and alcoholism are high among American Indians, leading to early death from cirrhosis of the liver. The high incidence of diabetes among Mexican Americans is caused in part by inappropriate diet. No data are available for the physical conditions of Asian Americans (Policy Issues Concerning the Elderly Minorities, 1979).

The incidence of mental illness is high among Mexican American elderly (Roberts, 1980; Newton and Ruiz, in press) and among blacks. With respect to elderly Asians, recent studies reported a higher incidence of psychosomatic illnesses secondary to stress. There are few data about the mental health of elderly American Indians (Rhoades et al., 1980), although the incidence of alchoholism is believed to be partly a consequence of the stress of acculturation (DeStefano et. al., 1979).

Mental health services must be made more available and responsive to the elderly because there are at least 100 different medical conditions which, if not treated promptly, may produce irreversible mental disorders. There is also a serious concern about the high incidence among the elderly of alcoholism which is usually associated with social isolation and depression. More programs dedicated to the prevention and treatment of the elderly alcoholic are needed, as this disease is the second most frequent admitting cause for hospitalizing elderly patients in a psychiatric facility (Busse and Pfeiffer, 1977). The incidence of mental illnesses increases with age, depression being one of the most common mental disorders in this group. Early intervention, diagnosis and treatment of depression could prevent 5000 to 8000 unnecessary deaths by suicide, or about 25 percent of all suicides in the nation reported in one year (Butler, 1978).

For elderly minorities, the causes for their lack of representation in mental health programs (under 4 percent) can be found in deficient outreach information and referral programs; lack of planning and coordination between mental health and social services agencies, bureaucracy and fragmentation of services; lack of input of minority leaders and the elderly themselves; programs which do not consider the barrio experience of this population; lack of bilingual, bicultural professional and paraprofessional staff; inaccessibility because of lack of transportaion and segregated housing patterns.

Social Services

Social services have failed to provide for the multiple needs of the minority elderly and their families. Even though their needs are greater, under utilization of services is the rule; existing services are inaccessible and governed by policies which are damaging to the elderly and their families. Two examples: the minority elderly are not allowed supplemental income at a functional age (55 years) comparable to that of the majority population. Because of their shorter life span a great number of minority elderly die before they become eligible for services. Only 50 percent of the Hispanic elderly, for example, receive SSI, compared to 75 percent of the general over 65-year-old population. Second, SSI programs discourage older persons from living in another person's household or having relatives moving in with them. For the minority elderly this means that they are deprived economically if they choose to be close to their natural support systems, those who provide more than 80 percent of their social and health needs. Thus, the elderly person is deprived emotionally because of isolation from relatives if he or she chooses to receive additional economic benefits.

The natural support systems of the elderly are disintegrating as a result of socioeconomic hardship and cultural stress; the all-giving and ever-present ethnic family seems to be an episode of the past (Moore, 1971). When appropriate social supports are provided, however, the families are helped once again to take care of their frail elders (Brody, S., 1978). There is also low utilization of informal associates in providing services to the client. These are more pleasing to elderly clients and less costly to the public (O'Brian, G. et al., 1980).

Social interactions among aged Hispanic and black elderly people are reduced because of their geographic isolation in neighborhoods of high crime and poor transportation (Creecy and Wright, 1979). Formal services reach only between 15 to 25 percent of the severely disabled elderly population. Minority groups are the most underserved: social service programs are organized without participation from minority-group professionals, caregivers, and community leaders; coordination and communication are absent between federal, state and local agencies; programs are inaccessible because of lack of transportation; outreach and information and referral programs are deficient; the minority elderly and their families are unaware of available resources; their census is undercounted (Policy Issues Concerning the Elderly Minorities, 1979); minority elderly fear and distrust federal programs because of past experience with discrimination (unfair immigration laws, broken treaties, and stereotypes); the unresolved cultural shock is still felt by many of the elderly minorities.

Aging males of minority groups are reluctant to seek public help because of pride, customs, traditions and social attitudes; it is also important to recognize that the elderly will first need to form a relationship of trust before they will provide information (Valle & Mendoza, 1978) and/or ask for help. Racial discrimination is a reality—race-neutral programs do not effectively meet the needs of the minority elderly (Future Directions for Aging Policies, 1980).

Living Arrangements

The minority elderly have great attachment to their homes and to the barrio and its subculture. They are fearful of being removed from their cultural surroundings and placed in institutions. When appropriate health and social services are provided in the community, the possiblity of remaining in the least restrictive environment (own home, foster home, congregate housing) increases

(Smyer, 1980). The choice of living arrangements will depend on the physical, social and environmental disabilities of the person. The nursing home may be adequate for some of the severely impaired elderly who need constant supervision and 24-hour medical and nursing care (Sloane and Gwyther, 1989).

The minority elderly are underrepresented in nursing homes. There is a need for multipurpose senior centers, foster care homes (Wymelemberg, 1980), for day-care centers in the community, and for congregate housing in the ethnic neighborhoods. Quality, availability and accessibility of living arrangements must be improved and research, policy and practice must be coordinated (Schultz, 1964).

Recommendations
Research
Action-oriented research is needed in areas of the natural support and health-delivery systems for the elderly minority group member.

Education
Knowledge through information of the specific ethnic characteristics of the minority groups is necessary for federal, state and local agencies. Service providers, professional/paraprofessionals would be sensitized to effective relations with the elderly if they were exposed to formal courses in gerontology and geriatrics with an ethnic perspective. Families and the elderly themselves can benefit if instruction is provided on such topics as how to deal with aging and losses and preparation for retirement. And finally, second-career training programs should be made available to the aged. There is a need to increase the number of minority professionals in the field of aging.

Health
Multipurpose, multidisciplinary health centers must be established in the community, with central coordination of health and social services and integration of available resources. those centers must provide assessment and case management (Eggert et al., 1980) and be involved not only in consultation, diagnosis, and treatment but also in primary prevention of high-risk diseases of the elderly. Such centers also need to offer mobile geriatric clinics which could reach the isolated frail elderly and provide case management and follow-up. The community mental health centers should design specific programs to attract a greater number of the elders.

Minority Participation
Minority participation in policymaking should be involved at federal, state and local levels.

Help for Families in Natural Support Systems
Technical and economic assistance should be given to self-support groups and families.

Census
Elders should be encouraged to participate in the census as allocation of

federal and state aid depends on the population counted; accessibility and utilization of social and health services should be improved by outreach and media programs and adequate transportation.

Housing and Living Arrangements

Aid for home repair and maintenance should be provided; number of ethnic housing and foster homes should be increased to prevent undue or unnecessary institutionalization and to facilitate access to nursing homes by the minority elderly when necessary.

SSI Programs

Insurance programs must be changed to prevent economic penalties for minority elderly who are living with relatives or having relatives move in with them (Annual Report to the President, 1979).

Eligibility of Public Benefits

At 55 years of age the minority elderly have the same functional deficits and mortality rates of 65-year-old white persons; public benefits for the minority elderly need to start at age 55.

Legal Aid

Crime prevention programs need to be made more available to the elder community in need.

An Ethnic Model of Long-Term Care

The treatment of a group of elderly Chinese opiate addicts in New York City (Deely et al., 1979) synthesized some useful characteristics of this model: the staff takes into consideration the ethnic characteristics, treats the clients with care, acceptance, respect, empathy and compassion. The caregiver becomes a new role model and a symbol of the family the elderly person may have lost.

Conclusion

The long-term care system is complicated by the politics of allocation of resources, negotiation of ppwer between institutions and professionals. The incidence of mental and physical disorders is higher in the minority elderly; nevertheless, there is underutilization of health and social services by this group. Inaccessibility of services is the result of a complex bureaucracy, uncoordination of services, geographic and cultural barriers. As natural support systems disintegrate because of economic and sociological changes, families and their elders experience despair and hopelessness. Lack of minority representation at the federal, state and local levels creates race-neutral programs which fail to serve the elderly. A centralized health/social system with easy access and cultural sensitivity appears to be an appropriate goal.

References

Brody, S.J. The Family care unit: A major consideraton in the long-term care support system. *Gerontologist*, 1978, *19*, 1969-1974.

Brody, E.M., et al., *A social work guide for long-term care facilities.* National Institute of Mental Health, U.S. Department of Health, Education, and Welfare, Public Health Service, Alcohol, Drug Abuse, and Mental Health Adminstration, 1977.

Bureau of the Census Current Population Reports, series P25 No. 311, July, 1965; and series P2J No. 704, July, 1977.

Busse, E.W., & Pfeiffer, E. *Mental illness in later life*, APA, Washington, D.C., 1973.

Busse, E.W., & Pfeiffer, E. Functional psychiatric disorders in old age. In *Behavior and adaptation in late life.* W. Busse & E. Pfeiffer, (Eds). Boston: Little, Brown & Company, 1977.

Butler, R., & Lewis, M. *Aging and mental health: Positive approaches.* St. Louis: C.-V. Mosley Co., 1973.

Butler R.N. *Why survive being old in America.* New York: Harper and Row, 1975.

Butler, R.N. *Overview on aging; The aging: The process and the people.* G. Usdin & C.K. Hofling (Eds). New York: Brunner/Mazel, 1978.

Cheah, K.C., Baldridge, J.A., & Beard, O.W. Geriatric evaluation unit of a medical service: Role of a geropsychiatrist. *Journal of Gerontology*, 1975, *1*, 41-45, 1975.

Creecy, R.F., & Wright, R. Morale and informal activity with friends among black and white elderly. *Gerontologist,* 1979, *19 (1)*, 544-547.

Deely, P.J., Kaufman, E., & Yen, S.M., et. al., The special problems and treatment of a group of elderly Chinese opiate addicts in New York City. *British Journal of Addiction*, 1979, *74*, 403-409.

DeStefano, F., Coulehan, J.L., & Wiant, K. Blood pressure survey on the Navajo Indian Reservation. *American Journal of Epidemiology*, 1979, *109 (3)*, 335-345.

Eggert, M.G., Bolyow, E., Nichols, J., & Carok, W. Gaining control of the long-term care system: First returns from the ACCESS experiment. *Gerontologist*, 1980, *20 (3)*, 356-363.

Federal Council on the Aging, Annual Report to the President. *Issues in long term care*, 1979.

Future directions for aging policies. A human service model report by the Select Committee on Aging, U.S. House of Representatives, 96th Congress, 2nd Session. Comm. Pub. No. 96, May, 1980.

Hanlon, J.J. Minority aging populations: Mortality and morbidity issues. In *Minority aging research: Old issues, new approaches.* E.P. Stanford (Ed). University Center on Aging, San Diego State University, 1975.

Johnson, J.J. *Minorities and aging.* Duke University Medical Center. Wadsworth Publishing Co., 1980.

Living arrangement options. In *The continuum of care*. Submitted by Policy/Planning Division, Office of Medical Programs, Texas Department of Human Resources, July 2, 1979.

Long-term care gerontology center delivery of services. Task Force Final Report, Texas Research Insititute of Mental Sciences, Houston, Texas, March 31, 1980.

Manton, K.G. Sex and race specific mortality differentials in multiple cause of death data. *Gerontologist*, 1980, *20 (4)*, 480-493.

Moore, J.W. Situational factors affecting minority aging. *Gerontologist*, 1971, *1*, 88-93.

Morris, R. Designing care for the long-term patient: How much change is necessary in the pattern of health provision? *American Journal of Public Health*, 1980, *70 (5)*, 470-472.

Newton, F.C., & Ruiz, R.A. Chicano culture and mental health among the elderly. In *Chicano aging and mental health*, M. Miranda and R.A. Ruiz (Eds.). Human Resources Corp., San Francisco, in press.

O'Brien, J.E. & Wagner, D.L. Help seeking by the frail elderly problems in network analysis. *Gerontologist*, 1980, *20 (1)*, 78-83.

Policy issues concerning the elderly minorities. A Staff Report, U.S. Department of Health and Human Services. The Federal Council on the Aging. DHHS Publication No. (OHDS) 80-20670, December, 1979.

Public policy and the frail elderly. A Staff Report, U.S. Department of Health Education and Welfare, Office of Human Development Services, Federal Council on Aging, Washington, D.C., December, 1978.

Raya, A.E. The minority aging: An action plan for health. *Minority aging and the legislative process*, E.P. Stanford (Ed.). University Center on Aging, San Diego State University, 1977.

Rhoades, E.R., Marshall, M., Attneave, C. et. al., Impact of mental disorders upon elderly American Indians as reflected in visits to ambulatory care facilities. *Journal of American Geriatric Society*, 1980, *8 (1)*, 33-39.

Roberts, R.E. Prevalence of psychological distress among Mexican Americans. *Journal of Health and Social Behavior*, 1980, *21*, 134-145.

Rose, D., Metsch, J.M., Moddy, H.R., et. al., The long-term challenge: Rationalizing a continuum of care for chronically impaired elderly. *Mount Sinai Journal of Medicine*, 1980, *2*, 87-95.

Schultz, A. *Studies in social theory* (Collected Papers 11), A. Broderson (Ed.). The Hague: Martinua Nijoff, 1964.

Sloane, P., & Gwyther, L. Nursing homes. *Journal of the American Medical Association*, 1980, *224 (16)*, 1840-1841.

Smyer, M.A. The differential usage of services by impaired elderly. *Journal of Gerontology*, 1980, *35 (2)*, 249-255.

Tate, N.P. *Ethnic considerations in service delivery to the minority aged in service delivery to the aged minorities*. J.N. Colen & D.L. Sota (Eds.). Funded through grants from Administrating on Aging, Washington D.C., 1979.

Southeastern New England Long-Term Care Gerontology Center. Notes from the Program in Medicine. *Rhode Island Medical Journal*, 1980, *63 (8)*, 283-284.

Valle, R., & Mendoza, L. *The elder Latino,* The Campanile Press, San Diego State University, 1978.

Wymelemberg, S. Foster homes another link to continuity—Long-term care. *Hospitals,* 1980, *54 (13)*, 61-63.

Azelia French-Upshaw, MSW-MPA
Office of Minority Services
California Department of Aging

IMPACT OF THE HUMAN SERVICES MODEL (OPTION SIX) ON LONG-TERM CARE

The human service model focuses on a continuum of care that makes services availablde to the individual as need increases or decreases. Some advocates of long-term care welcome the model as it de-emphasized the medical factor traditionally associated with long-term care. Reflecting on some of the earlier advocacy trends for the provision of services, the model responds to some of the issues that plagued administrators of institutions of care providing facilities—adequate resources to cover the cost of providing care. Also, the model projects the theory of serving the whole person—meeting the individual's psycho-social, physical and economic needs. Thus, family, friends, religious affiliates and culture groups are included in the delivery system.

Earlier supporters of long-term care facilities referred to the model as geriatric care. Such a model carried the philosophy that the institution was not necessarily the last place to go before death, but rather a focal point for specialized services to enable one to move back and forth "in" the community. The model provides for ancillary or supportive services to the extent necessary to remain in the community. Under the geriatric care model, specialists based in the institution would be expected to provide technical assistance to service providers in the community. Community services would be placed in satellites from the institution. Earlier advocates for this model felt that it could bridge the gap between "need" and "security" of specialized, professional staff and that it could be cost effective. They supported it as a supplement to institutional care. Authorities advocating in behalf of older minorities, however, have stated that the problem for older minority persons is "not how to keep minorities out of an institution, but rather how to get into an adequate, acceptable and accessible institution when they need care." To the extent that the model will make resources available to maintain adequate, acceptable, accessible community-based institutions for older minorities, the model represents a positive factor. Whether the focal point of services is called a multiservice center with a component for acute or chronic care, or a geriatric center, may actually be insignificant. The significant factor is the availability of the service in the community—adequately and appropriately meeting the total needs of the older minority person.

Should Policy Making and Service Provision be Centralized or Decentralized in the Model

Response

The model emphasized decentralization—a return to local authority—wherever possible for planning coordination and delivery of human services. The report indicates that " . . . the system mandates whatever is needed to return limited fiscal resources directly to those involved in the service event—seniors in need and service providers." If it could be found that existing service-delivery systems were set up based on clearly identified "needs," and services are placed in areas where there are the greatest social and economic needs; that "need" was established by a universal norm; and if it could be established that service providers were representative of the ethnic minority in need of a respective service; and, if adequate representation of all communities were required among policy makers, then decentralized policy making would be a positive factor for older minority persons. However, experience with local planning and coordinating agencies responsible for developing service delivery systems has generally required the authority of state and local governments to provide equitable and appropriate services to minority people.

The 1978 Amendments to the Older Americans Act mandates that local Area Agencies on Aging plan and develop a service delivery system that meets the needs of older Americans, and that priority for receipt of these services be those with the greatest social and economic needs. In many areas, "needs" have not been adequately identified and services have not been provided those with greatest need, but rather in areas where the greatest pressure for services have come.

James F. Loschiano writing in *Journal of Minority Aging*, 1978, indicates three types of need criteria—normative need, felt need and prior receipt of service. Normative need is described as that which the expert or professional defines as needed in any given situation. A standard is laid down and compared with the existing standards. Felt need is equated with want. When needs are assessed for services the population is asked if it needs it. Prior receipt of service need occurs when the need for services within a current time period is equated with receipt of service in a previous time period.

Needs-assessment of older minority persons as well as the overall older population is usually an area of gross neglect at the local, as well as state level. Where area agencies have completed need assessments, they have usually been based on "felt need". With "felt need" as the basis for service, consider a statement made by an older black man—"Growing old means a lot of sacrifices, however, when you're black you're accustomed to it." Sacrifice, neglect and inequity are experiences of most older minority people. They have learned to live without and adjust to the situation. Planning programs based on "felt needs" are inadequate to meet the normative needs of older minority persons who have, through necessity, learned to control their "wants". Local policy makers have traditionally been unable to withstand the political pressures that promote inequity of services for minorities, and older minority persons have generally been inactive participants in the policy making process.

Once a service is developed in an area, a need has been established. Poorly planned service delivery points establish needs where normative need may not exist. Where service delivery points have been poorly defined and programs exist in areas that have low priority of need, program planners at the local level may continue to bypass those with the greatest social and economic needs. Limited resources available in a community that has not identified and planned for needs of older minority persons, may mean continued inequity and/or lack of service.

Although the human service model places a strong emphasis on "need," and true need must be defined at the local level, local strategies for determining need usually work against older minority persons. Traditionally, it has been recognized that to insure equity in policy making and service delivery for older minority persons, local policy makers need the "strong arm" of state and federal governments.

Sharon Y. Moriwaki, Ph.D.
Program Administrator
Department of Labor and Industrial Relations
State of Hawaii

EMPLOYMENT

The Older Americans Act affirms the right of all older people to "an adequate income in retirement, " "employment with no discriminatory personnel practices because of age," and "meaningful employment opportunities." To assess whether the act has improved the life for minority eldrers, let us first look briefly at some of the statistics on income and employment:

Income
One of the major problems encountered in the later years particularly after age 65 is that of living on a drastically curtailed income. For example, the proportion of the total population (including familes and unrelated individuals) who had incomes below the poverty level in 1975 was 12.3 percent. In contrast, among those 65 years and older, 15.3 percent were living below the poverty level. For minority elderly, the problem was even more severe, with 36.3 percent of the black elders over 65 having incomes below the poverty lvel (NCOA, *Factbook on Aging* figures from U.S. Census, February 1978:44).

Adding to the problem of fixed incomes, continually rising health care and other costs, and the longer period of life after retirement have placed an ever greater strain on the retired person's resources. Thus, maintaining an adequate income throughout old age is a major problem.

Employment
The lower incomes of minority elderly can be seen as a result of discrimination in the labor force during their younger years. For example, in 1975 the unemployment statistics indicate that for all age groups 35 years and older, minorities were more likely to be unemployed. The unemployment rate of males aged 45-54 years was 4.4 percent for whites but was twice as high for minorities—9.0 percent. Although those age 55 and older were less likely to be in the labor force and looking for work, the unemployment rate was still higher for minority elderly males—6.1 percent as compared to 4.1 percent for their white counterparts (Employment and Training Report of the President, 1977).

Many elders are working to meet their financial and other needs. In 1975,

2.6 million persons over 62 were working, of whom only 11 percent were non-white. However, the incomes of those aged 65 and older who were working were much lower than those aged 40 to 64. The mean annual earnings of those 65 and older was about a half the income of those aged 45-64—$6,505 as compared to $10,964. The income for black elders aged 65 and older was even lower at $3,694. For both black and white alike, women over age 65 had incomes disproportionately lower than men. Thus, even when working, incomes were not adequate for our minority elders.

The Report of the Congressional Subcommittee on Human Services pointed to the need for a human service model for the future based on a strong economic strategy. Employment for the elderly then could be seen as a critical component not only in terms of meeting financial needs but also in terms of providing opportunities for meaningful activities and involvement in the mainstream society. Such a national policy was also discussed at the meetings of our national White House conference Technical Committee on Employment. We focused on the necessity for a national policy that seeks to retain older workers who are contributing their skills and experience, and to encourage government, employers and unions to reassess current policies which provide disincentives to work. There are thus two levels of concern: 1) policies regarding retention of older persons who are currently working; and 2) the creation of meaningful jobs for the older person who has been out of the labor force but wants or needs to return. Employment and retirement are basically interrelated. The size and adequacy of retirement income depend largely on the size and continuity of income in the years before retirement. Low earnings, underemployment or frequent unemployment in the working years, as experienced by many of our minority populations, cut down on the amount which can be saved or credited toward a retirement income.

Major emphasis must thus be placed on policies and practices to provide full opportunity for workers in their 40's and 50's who need jobs to support themselves and their familes now, but also need to build up their credits for future retirement benefits. Our policy should also create options for those 60 and older, with employment opportunities for those who need or want to work as well as pension and/or entitlement programs for others who want to leave the work force on an adequate income.

The minority elderly are especially vulnerable in that they are restricted in their options. They generally had lower earnings during their work life, which results in lower social security benefits in retirement, or none at all for some. They have generally been in low-skilled occupations or in arduous jobs where they can no longer remain as they grow older, nor do they want to. As one older Filipino gentleman put it, "I worked in the hot sun all my life; I don't want to go back to that—but I don't know anything else."

What options for employment do these elders have? Two federal employment programs, the Comprehensive Employment and Training Act (CETA) and Senior Community Service Employment Program (SCSEP) are focused on the needs of the vulnerable population.

CETA's mandate since its inception included the elderly as a target group; however, the prime sponsor system has not been providing a consistently acceptable level of services to this significant segment. For example, under Title I (for training and retraining of the hard-core unemployed), of the total clients served in 1978, only 4.4 percent were 45 to 54 years of age, with a lower proportion, 3.3 percent over 55 years of age. For public service employment, Title II D (transitional employment opportunities) and Title VI (counter cyclical employment), the service levels were 8.9 percent and 8.3 percent respectively for those 45 to 54 years of age, and 5.6 percent and 5.2 percent respectively for those over 55 years of age.

Notwithstanding these low figures on service to the elderly under CETA, older workers constitute about one-third of the civilian labor force, and, up until age 65, their labor force participation rate was 13.27 percent in 1976, a high figure given the pressures toward retirement that existed at that time. (Employment and Training Report of the President, 1977). One can conclude then, that prior to the 1978 amendments, older workers were not getting their fair share of CETA training and PSE slots.

There were no statistics available by ethnic group for CETA participants. However, with the proposed directives of the new administration, we can expect that minority elderly will be negatively affected. PSE Titles IID and VI have had a higher rate of participation by the elderly than have any of the other CETA programs; however, these two programs are expected to be phased out by September 30, 1981. On the other hand, Title VII (Private Sector Initiative Program), least successful in serving elders in general, is expected to grow. Based on past experience, this program lodged in the private sector portends a poor outlook for minority elderly participation.

Senior Community Service Employment Program (SCSEP)

Because of the emphasis on youth in current CETA programming, the most likely route for elderly employment would be the expansion of the Senior Community Service Employment Program (SCSEP) under Title V of the Older Americans Act. However, it is funded at a much lower level than CETA. In FY80, Title V receives a total national allocation of 258 million dollars, as compared to 8.1 billion dollars received by CETA. SCSEP provides approximately 56,000 (1979-80) part-time public service jobs for economically disadvantaged older workers who are 55 years of age and older. It thus serves only 1 percent of the estimated five million eligible economically disadvantaged older workers.

Although the impact in terms of numbers is not great, SCSEP has made efforts to include minority participants; in 1979-80, 32.5 percent of its total participants were non-white (see Table 1.).

Although SCSEP has served well the ethnic elderly aged 55 and older who are most in need, it is obvious that the funding level is so low that the program has had negligible impact in terms of the large segment of our minority elderly population who want or need to work. One of our SCSEP contractors in Hawaii has 132 slots, all filled, with an equal number on his waiting list. The problem here is that of providing hope and expectations among the segment of our population that has been discouraged in the job market for so long. We raise their

Table 1.

Total Participants Served Under SCSEP, 1979-80*

Ethnic Group	No.	%
White	38,257	67.5
Black	12,228	21.6
Hispanic	3,590	6.3
Indian/Alaskan	1,376	2.4
Asian/Pacific	1,210	2.1
Total	56,661	100.0

*Source: Office of National Programs for Older Workers, U.S. DoI, Employment and Training Administration, Washington, D.C.

expectations, but once again they are on waiting lists with no outcomes.

In addition to the limited number of jobs available in relation to need is the current policy of allocating most of the funds to national organizations. In 1979-80, 80.6 percent of the funds were awarded to national organizations, and of this amount only 4.5 percent was awarded to specific minority organizations.

In our efforts to employ older workers, state employment offices have been called upon to counsel and place older workers. However, perhaps due to their having to serve nine other priority target groups, their placement rates have been below that for applicants in general. For example, in Hawaii the total placement rate was 20 percent, whereas, for applicants aged 45 to 64 it was 12 percent, and for those aged 65 and over it was only 10 percent. If SCSEP, with its limited funding, is to be used effectively, perhaps thought should be given to allocating a larger portion of funds to the states to enable them to develop more jobs for their older populations.

Additionally, as we move into a decade which is directed toward less government spending, cost-containment and cutbacks in human services, we should reassess the Title V exclusion of the private sector. Although the goal is unsubsidized placement, the majority of SCSEP slots are in community service agencies which have limited funding—and will perhaps have even less in the future—and poor prospects for providing unsubsidized jobs for elders. What is needed is the involvement of the private sector. The current regulations, by excluding placements in profit making organizations, restrict our placing older persons in the workplace where they can prove their merits and consequently be hired on in unsubsidized jobs.

In short, SCSEP, although necessary and successful in providing meaningful opportunities and income for the disadvantage elderly who are fortunate enough to participate, is a short-raange, "band-aid" solution to the problem of employment for minority elders.

More comprehensive policies and programs need to be developed in addition to expanding SCSEP via placements in the private sector. We need older worker retraining and retention programs, with accompanying tax incentives to employers, greater emphasis on job creation and development, and efforts toward developing age-neutral job requirements. Greater attention should be given to assessing the skills, experiences and interests of older workers as well as the specific skills and requirements needed by employers. The critical element is an effective match between employers' needs and older workers' skills— without which negative stereotypes regarding older workers will not be changed.

In addition, not only the employment, but just as importantly, the education sector must be encouraged to provide vocational programs for the elderly. Community colleges, universities and adult education programs need to look upon the vocational needs of the older worker, rather than, as is currently being done, looking only to satisfy their avocational needs. If we are to change employers' attitudes toward hiring older workers, efforts must be placed on training as well. Employers can be persuaded to hire or retain older workers on their performance alone rather than age. On the other hand, we must not overlook the sometimes very real problem expressed by employers who have been reluctant to hire older workers for fear of age discrimination suits should these older workers be terminated due to their failure to perform satisfactorily. Such fears can be assuaged through more effective job matching and counseling, but more importantly, through training.

The older Americans Act, then, should be more strongly advocacy-oriented in its efforts on all fronts—in schools, in the workplace, in employment agencies, with unions, as well as in the community—so that doors will be opened to the elderly worker or potential worker. The bottom line in employment for the elderly is that they be given equal opportunity for training/retraining as well as for suitable jobs.

David C. Pritchard, Ph.D.
Lory Y. Kitamura, MSW Candidate
School of Social Work
San Diego State University

MINORITY AGING INPUT
IN INSTITUTIONS OF HIGHER EDUCATION

Introduction

Minority aging issues and input in the field of education and training is an ongoing concern within institutions of higher education, as minority aging-related priorities and recommendations have been documented time and again. However, given the current political and economic climate, this concern may remain primarily an academic question as policymakers respond to budgetary constraints of the current administration. In response to the 1981 White House Conference on Aging, various individuals and groups within and outside minority communities are preparing to confront the vitally important issues which affect minority elderly; however, resolutions and recommendations, although just and responsive to a significant need, cannot be based solely on the reliance of government expenditures for implementation of policy. A key issue is that of developing strategies to implement policy which assure minority aging input in the area of education/training, but such strategies must develop beyond academic and political rhetoric which cites the fiscal responsibilities of the federal government.

Gerontological education and training has developed rapidly in response to a rising public concern regarding the condition of the growing number of elderly; however, disciplines in higher education have inadequately addressed minority aging issues and concerns in their curricula. A framework needs to be developed which assumes the importance of cultural pluralism and socio-cultural differences (Langston, 1979). The integration of ethnic minority content would significantly improve gerontological curricula. Supporters of minority aging curriculum development base their arguments on an underlying philosophy which states:

1. a concern for the need to provide knowledge of ethnic minority groups for faculty, practitioners and students in helping professions in aging from a multi-cultural perspective;

2. a concern for expanding the knowledge base in minority aging which in turn affects program development and service delivery); and,

3.   a concern for the need to train a greater number of ethnic educators and practitioners in the helping professions. (Stanford, 1975,
p. 56)

To put these concerns in perspective, it is important to examine the role the
federal government has played in the current status of minority aging-oriented
education/training, as well as the status of minority input in course content/
training provisions in gerontological education and related disciplines in institutions of higher education.

Federal Policy

Federal policy in aging, embodied in the Older Americans Act (as amend-
ed in 1978), fails to address minority aging input in its provisions for education/
training. According to the Federal Council on Aging/Special Aging Committee's
Report (1972, p.42), federal aging policies "do not provide for sufficient funds
to minority universities for minority personnel training, nor for advocacy or research in the field of minority aging." One can argue further that beyond federal
policies' failure to provide sufficient funding, the legislation is basically "minority-
blind" and does not specifically acknowledge minority aging issues in education/
training. As a result, gerontology programs in higher education have not been
sufficiently responsive in respect to minority aging input.

Curriculum Development

A survey of course titles and descriptions of educational programs in gerontology reveals: 1) few courses which integrate minority issues, and 2) an
absence of courses specifically addressing minority aging issues. (AGHE, 1976)
to prepare professionals and others to provide direct services to elderly and
specifically minority elderly. These professionals include social workers, psychologists, a range of health care personnel, counselors, recreation specialists, etc.
In addition, other disciplines will have significant impact on minority elderly
but in indirect ways, i.e., architecture, public administration, geography, business,
urban studies, political science, etc. Graduates from these programs become involved in planning, research, policy developments and administrative activies
affecting older persons.

Although more aging courses are being incorporated into the curricula,
the process continues to be fragmented, and many colleges and universities are
turning out graduates in the helping professions, who will be working in some
capacity with elderly consumers, without having had specific courses in gerontology. In respect to minority aging, the gerontological curricula being offered contains insufficient minority content. To correct this situation requires a
more enlightened curriculum development process as well as the effort to
expand the knowledge base in the area of minority aging to provide additional
data for curriculum building.

In a related area, there is a need for more minority individuals to assume
roles in gerontological educaiton. Higher educational institutions have been
remiss in not making more substantial efforts to recruit and train minority
persons for several important responsibilities: 1) as students to become helping
professionals to work directly with minority aging populations; 2) as educators

and trainers to provide needed cultural perspectives and to assume leadership roles; and 3) as researchers to conduct minority specific research in aging.

Extracurricular Program Needs

In addition to increasing minority content in the curriculum and recruiting minority students and educators, institutions of higher educaiton can perform additional functions to further support the minority elderly population:

1.   Involve minority elderly as learners.   Participation as learners in educational programs is a creative and meaningful activity for retired persons.   Universities and colleges need to reach out both to attract minority elderly to their campuses and to offer courses and programs in more familiar surroundings off campus. Traditional barriers which too often preclude participation need to be lowered.

2.   Involve minority elderly in service roles.   Another feasible and useful role for minority older persons relates to the different possibilities for stimulating voluntary involvement which higher education can offer.   Some examples include: as resource persons who can share personal aging experiences from culturally diverse backgrounds in classrooms, on research and training projects, and in inter-generational and cross-cultural programs; as research assistants gathering data in ethnic communities; serving on committees, advisory boards and councils as community representatives; as volunteers or paid staff in different departments or services.

3.   Provision of retirement education.   Insufficient attention has been focused on retirement roles and possibilities for minority elderly. Although basic survival needs command first priority, the quality of retirement living and the satisfaction experienced are also very important.   Institutions of higher education can play a useful role in this vital area.   The basic problem is that many retired persons, including many minority elderly, have not participated in formal pre-retirement planning programs.   This population, not covered by industrial or government retirement education programs, have not been stimulated to plan and prepare for retirement activities, social relationships, and new roles. Higher education can develop outreach strategies and retirement education programs to impact this population.

Recommendations

If substantial changes are to occur in these different areas, efforts need to go forward on several fronts.   The White House Conference on Aging can accelerate these initiatives by highlighting the issues and needed policy changes, and can alert those individuals, organizations and institutions which can play a facilitating role in bringing about change.   The following strategies are recommended:

1. To propose specific changes in the Older Americans Act to empha-
    size the importance of minority-oriented gerontological curriculum
    and to provide incentives for educating and training minority stu-
    dents for professional roles;

2. To obtain support for leadership at the national level from govern-
    ment agencies, i.e., AOA, NIA, and professional organizations,
    i.e., Gerontological Society, AGHE, to influence institutions of
    higher education to put greater emphasis on gerontological curri-
    culum with inclusion of minority aging content, to make greater
    recruitment efforts for minority students in gerontology programs,
    and to involve minority elderly in learning and service roles;

3. To recommend policy development related to the need for retire-
    ment education programs for those individuals, including many
    minority elderly, not served by industrial or government pre-retire-
    ment programs.

References

Association for Gerontology in Higher Education. *National directory of educational pro-
    grams in gerontology.* Washington, D.C.: Department of Health, Education and
    Welfare, 1976.

Federal Council on Aging. *Policy issues concerning the elderly minorities.* Washington,
    D.C.: Department of Health and Welfare, 1979.

Langston, E.J. Community involvement and research. In E.P. Stanford (Ed.), *Minority
    aging research: Old issues, new approaches.* University Center on Aging, San Diego
    State University, 1979.

Stanford, E.P. (Ed.). Curriculum workshop. *Proceedings of the Second Institute on Minor-
    ity Aging.* Center on Aging, San Diego State University, 1975.

IV

Special Concerns

Lodis Rhodes, Ph.D.
LBJ School of Public Affairs
University of Texas at Austin

INCOME NEEDS OF MINORITY AGED

Any attempt to determine the income needs of the minority aged will invariably be more academic than practical for two reasons. First, the current art of microeconomic analysis is more properly relegated to the pages of professional journals than it is to reliably predicting how much money minority elders need to meet their individual needs. Second, I have yet to hear a convincing argument that our normative definition of the poverty level—the money required for a non-farm family of four to maintain a basic standard of living—has a meaningful relationship to how individuals spend money. My suspicion is that analysts like the poverty index because it can be used to generate other figures they can play with and over which they can argue the soundness of their analytic techniques. There is little quesitons that the index, because it is artificially low, has the effect of underestimating the number of individuals who are ill-clothed, housed, and fed. Needless to say, minority elders have special problems in generating the post-retirement incomes to meet their needs adequately. We do not have very good income data on the currently retired minority aged, and poor data measured against an index that has little real meaning merely compounds the problem of setting budget levels. Since current income data and analytic techniques are not likely to produce a picture of spending which accurately reflects the budget practices of most minority elders, I will leave the task of debating what those budget levels should be to others in favor of outlining how differing interpretations of income and what it means to be old influence policymakers in their design of programs for the elderly.

Publicly supported programs for the elderly have sought to meet an often confusing blend of economic and social objectives. At times we seem to be motivated by some "humanitarian" impulse to help the elderly, usually because we have assumed that they cannot help themselves. At other times our actions have little or nothing to do with enabling the elderly to help themselves. We become cost conscious and unwilling to spend money for some programs. Some of our policy and program efforts have proved to be curious, ineffective blends of our schizophrenic tendencies. Even staunch supporters of programming for the elderly have not always been able or willing to clearly separate the economic from the socio-psychological objectives they seek to achieve through various programs. This is certainly revealed in recent debates about the economic and social conditions faced by the minority aged. The empirical task is to determine which aspects of the life circumstances of the minority aged are primarily atttributable to being a member of minority ethnic group, and which are caused by being a particular age. It is not an easy task, but one which analysts with a special interest in the plight of the minority aged can and must begin doing better. One area where we can improve despite the limitations of current data is in analyzing income and work profiles as they relate to retirement and pension policies. My point here is a simple one: any effort to say anything meaningful about post-retirement income must be said and understood within the context of sound analyses of preretirement employment and income profiles. Further, since retirement is an imposed social characteristic, it becomes even more important to be able to separate the economic from the soci-psychological considerations when discussing and setting budget levels.

Income and Being Old

Policymakers must know the difference between two distinct concepts when they analyze and set budget levels. One is *income* and the other is *being old*. The concepts take on some unusual relationships in the publicly-supported programs for the elderly, sometimes because supporters of programs have not always been able to separate clearly the economic and social objectives of various programs. The distinction is important in an era when policymakers seem to ask what programs cost and who pays before asking what they are supposed to do. Those who support particular programs must be able to give more precise answers to questions about the immediate and long-term cost of programs and whether policy changes are intended to benefit current or future cohorts of minority aged. Better answers will be found from generating and analysing income profiles of the working population.

I can think of five reasons why policymakers want to know the income level of an individual or family. First, level of income is a fairly reliable indicator of wealth for most of us because our net worth is usually the wages we are paid minus tax payments. A second reason income level is important to policymakers is that it provides an imprecise although useful measure of whether a person has enough money to buy basic goods and services. A third and more relevant reason to know income levels is that they used to establish eligibility for participating in publicly-supported, means-tested service programs. Because we need to know what it will cost to support current programs in future years, current income levels when used with other socioeconomic data such as age and education can be used to predict future income levels for an individual. Finally, income level, when coupled with other socioeconomic data, can be current income levels when used with other socioeconomic data such as age and education can be used to predict future income levels for an individual. Finally, income level, when coupled with other socioeconomic data, can be used to evaluate whether work opportunities and income have been fairly dis-Policymakers emphasize different reasons at different times to justify their actions. Clearly, the last three reasons are of particular importance to policymakers as they debate the economic plight of the elderly. They need to know how many people will be immediately eligible and likely to participate in a new program; if that number (and thus the cost) will increase in future years; and if the program favors a subgroup of the target population now or at some future date. I will return to how these three considerations and their relationship to post-retirement income in a moment, but first I need to introduce the second concept with which analysts must grapple when they try to evaluate the life circumstance of the minority aged.

The second concept is a sociological one: being old. Being old is often confused with chronological age. The two are not the same, although as one ages one will likely take on or have imposed those social and psychological characteristics which we define as being old. Simply stated, being old implies that a person cannot effectively carry out his or her daily activities. Even more important here is the connection that we make between being old (i.e., inability to cope) and retirement. The connection implicitly and unfortunately blends socio-psychological with economic considerations. It does so by equating the period during which one receives income from sources other than wages with being unable to cope. Simply stated: one is retired because he or she is expected to quickly become a less efficient worker than one who is younger. This reasoning, of course, implies that a younger worker will do an equal or better job for less cost. Connecting being old—the inability to carry out daily activities—with being retired—the absence of wage-generated income—is to confuse a socio-psychological concept with an economic one. As a result, it is easy to make the mistake of basing socio-psychological assessments of the elderly on economic data. This is clearly the pitfall which must be avoided when one sets out to analyze the income and budgetary needs of the minority aged.

Pre- and Post-Retirement Incomes of the Minority Aged

Employment and retirement are economic concepts which describe participation in the labor force. How one participates in the labor force is a pretty direct measure of the income a person is likely to receive during those years of working and of retirement. I must quickly add that work in and of itself has little to do with employment or retirement, and that what we recognize as the labor force includes neither all workers nor all who want to work. The labor force is in fact a combination of occupations and professions which have been certified as legitimate through various social and political institutions. The same institutions, primarily schools and training programs, then certify some individuals as being qualified to hold those jobs. How and which workers are certified set the demographic characteristics of the labor force. If some potential workers are excluded from training and educational opportunities, the chances are higher that they will be excluded as well from the labor force. The result is that the excluded groups will have an unstable employment record and no source of steady, wage-generated income. Although I have oversimplified the relationship which exists between education and training as certification devices, that relationship partially explains why blacks and other minorities have been at a distinct disadvantage in competing for jobs in the labor force. The disadvantage from the employment years extends into retirement. The disadvantage translates into lower levels of lifetime incomes and sometimes unreliable sources of income during both the working and the retired years.

Although it seems to be an obvious and straightforward statement, post-retirement income for salaried employees is directly determined by the sources and amount of pre-retirement income. However, predicting levels of post-retirement income from pre-retirement sources is difficult for several reasons. Different groups in the population acquire income in different ways, with cash income generated from a salaried job being but one source of income. As previously mentioned, most of us derive income from a salaried job, although in point of fact income is generated from many sources; by interest earned on saving, earnings from assets (personal and real property), cash gifts and cash payments and in-kind benefits from public programs. In addition, potential sources of income might include the personal and real property which a person might own. Not only is it difficult to survey and calculate total income for people who receive money from multiple sources during pre-retirement work years, those sources produce different proportions of a person's income at different times in his or her life. For example, some assets are more easily converted to cash than others; some pre-retirement assets will not produce available income until after retirement.

It is difficult to calculate the disposable income available to a person from these different income sources. It is even more difficult to predict how sources of income might change over time for an individual or ethnic group. For example, the sources of income for blacks who are currently retired may differ from the sources of income for those who will retire in the future, primarily because young workers have employment opportunities which their parents or grandparents were denied. One then can reasonably expect that their retirement incomes will differ in kind and amount from that of their parents and grandparents. Analyzing income in this context is more complicated than measuring income against the poverty level, the usual method of comparing retirement incomes of different groups. The comparison masks the effect cash and potential cash income from other sources have a disposable retirement income. If we cannot or have not established income profiles for the age and ethnic cohorts we are interested in, we are left to speculate about post-retirement income for them.

I indicated earlier that we do not have good income data for the population. The data available which pertains to members of ethnic groups is of poorer quality than the aggregate data, primarily because it was not gathered in a way which permits us to answer the income questions we ask about particular ethnic groups. Our income analyses suffer from the well-known limitations imposed by using aggregate population data (census and/or social security tapes) to answer questions about specific groups comprising that population. The fact is that relatively better income data is available for males than females; for whites than blacks; for whites and blacks than other ethnic groups; and the working rather than the retired. Despite these limitations, one can begin to shape a picture of the relative income status of blacks and whites who are retired or near retirement. I must caution that the picture developed is one of relationships between incomes, and it shows only a snapshot in time of segments of the population. Moreover, the members of ethnic groups in the data files may not represent the target populations of interest to us for the reasons just cited—the differences within and across ethnic groups may differ significantly from those which are revealed when comparing the incomes of cohorts or black and white males.

Those who are at or near retirement must rely heavily on pension benefits for their post-retirement income. Over two-thirds of currently retired individuals receive at least 50 percent of their income from pensions, public and private; one-third receive more than 90 percent of their income from these programs. There is no reason to believe that the percentage will not increase given the participation rates of current workers in pension programs. Because past employment practices restricted blacks to marginal work and career opportunities, with the income effect being both lower pay and lifetime earnings, one can surmise that they are over represented in that group for which benefits comprise more than 90 percent of its income. To the degree that black retirees must rely on pension benefits for their income, they hover below the 1979 poverty level of $3,479 to $4,390 for those at least 65 years old.

Median family income rose by 6.7 percent during the 1970s. The current median income for a family of four is $19,684 compared with a 1970 figure of $18,444 ($9,867 in 1970 dollars). The 1970 poverty index for that family is $7,386. Poverty as measured by the index did not change significantly during the decade, *except for the elderly and two-parent black families*. The exceptions not surprisingly include the population of interest to us. A higher percentage of those at least 65 years old were below the poverty level of $3,472 ($4,363 for a married couple) than in 1970 and more two-parent black couple families were poor in 1979 than in 1970. Moreover, persons living in the inner city were twice as likely to be poor than those in farm/rural areas. These figures paint a bleak income picture for blacks in general, and in particular for black elders who live in urban areas. Although it is significant that more currently retired workers dropped below the poverty level during the study period, that fact may not be as significant as the income patterns of younger two-parent black families and middle-aged (50-64) black workers.

If currently retired blacks are poorer now than they were ten years ago, the picture for soon-to-retire blacks is equally bleak. A comparison of employment and earnings profile of midle-aged (50-64) black and white males shows that blacks earn less and have more erratic employment records than whites. Both patterns will translate into lower post-retirement incomes for blacks, a prospect for them which is fact for the currently retired. Middle-aged black workers make 68 percent as much as white workers. This income ratio held steady during the five year study period (1966-71). While both whites and blacks will become poorer during retirement, the pattern indicates that blacks will be poorer than the norm (Current Population Reports, 1980; Abbott, 1980).

The three income profiles for younger two-parent black families; middle-aged black male workers; and currently retired blacks show that they lag behind whites and are closer to the poverty level in all demographic groupings. The pictures lack the detail to support anything but the most general statements about income status and how it affects our subjective opinions of the social well-being of minority elders. What is clear from the pictures is that those at least 65 years old have less real income now than ten years ago, and they were poor by any standard at that time. Black retirees are poorer and the economic picture changes very little for them from working to retirement years. I mean by this that blacks must continue to use their lifelong skill of getting the most value from their relative few shrinking dollars. What also should be clear from the pictures is that the income data which we do have not a meaningful or valid basis for arguing that black retirees *feel* less economically secure or less confident than their white counterparts. I suspect that just the opposite is true. If so, we must develop and use more specialized income data and sharply-honed philosophical arguments for why and how the very real income gaps should be closed, and government policy is the only reasonable tool to use in closing it.

References

Abbot, J. Work experience and earnings of middle-aged black and white men, 1965-71. *Social Security Bulletin*, December, 1980, *43, (12)*.

Current Population Reports (1980). *Money income and poverty status of families and persons in the United States: 1979* (Advance Report). Bureau of the Census: U.S. Department of Commerce. October. Series P-60, No. 125.

Martha B. McFadden, M.A.
University Center on Aging
San Diego State University

THE IMPACT OF INCREASING THE NATIONAL AGE OF RETIREMENT ON THE MINORITY ELDERLY

In preparation for the 1981 White House Conference on Aging, it is appropriate that we turn our attention to those programs and policies which have significant impact on the quality of life for older members of minority groups. This paper will focus on a single proposal for alteration of policy which, if accepted by legislators, will have far-reaching consequences for minority elders. Specifically, I will address recommendations by the Advisory Council on Social Security for a phased increase in the age of full entitlement for Social Security retirement benefits.

Since 1900 the number of elderly in the United States has increased dramatically, representing a larger share of the total population for each succeeding decade. Between 1900 and 1970 the total United States population grew almost threefold while the elderly segment (persons aged 65 and over) grew almost sevenfold (Brotman, 1978). This trend is expected to continue with projections indicating that by 2030, 18.3 percent of the total United States population will be 64 years of age or over. The growth of the elderly population in both numbers and proportion can be attributed to increased longevity (Rhine, 1978), the movement of the post-World War II baby boom through the population pyramid, and declining fertility rates (Feldstein, 1975). The combination and interactive effects of these trends are bring us an aging society with an increasing median age.

The implications of an expanding elderly population on employment patterns and related policy issues are varied and complex. During the past two decades one of the most significant developments in our nations's work scene has been the accelerated pace at which older men and women have been leaving the work place, either voluntarily or involuntarily. Labor force projections for 1990 indicate that persons age 55 and over, and particularly those over 65, will show an increased preference for leisure over work (Flaim and Fullerton, 1979).

In 1970, the Department of Labor figures indicated that less than 40.7 percent of males aged 65 to 69 remained in the labor force. In 1980 this proportion was 35.5 percent and in 1990 it will be 33.6 percent.

Related to declining labor force participation is a growing trend toward early retirement (Quinn, 1977; Sheppard and Rix, 1977; Spengler, 1975). A dramatic illustration of this accelerating trend is the fact that in 1974, 64 percent of retired workers receiving newly awarded benefits were persons under 65 and seeking reduced benefits available to retires at ages 62 through 64. In contrast, in 1961, only 21 percent of retired workers receiving newly awarded benefits were under 65 years of age (Campbell, 1977). By 1976, 75 percent of all workers applying for Social Security sought reduced benefits available to retirees at age 62 (Singer, 1978). When one considers all retiring employees and not just Social Security beneficiaries, the trend toward early retirement is even more dramatic. In 1976, of all retiring employees, 90 percent were younger than 65 (Newsletter of the Case Center for Gerontological Studies, 1979).

The current trend toward early retirement, coupled with the present and projected age structure in the United States, has significant macroeconomic implications. The combination of these factors leads us to expect a ballooning in the percentage of retired persons through the middle of the next century. The impact of this growing retired population can be assessed in terms of its effect on the dependency ratio (Clark and Spengler, 1978).

The dependency ratio is the ratio of non-workers to workers in a society. The old-age-dependency ratio (dependency ratio for persons 65 and older) increases when either the working group decreases in size or the non-working group increases in size. Most discussions of age structure effects on the dependency ration point toward the dual concepts of increased proportions of elderly and decreased proportions of persons under 20 years of age. In their totality, these phenomena are offsetting until 2020, when the post-World War II babies will reach retirement age. Between 1973 and 2030 we can expect a 67 percent increase in the old-age-dependency ratio. This substantial increase can, in part be attributed to the fact that by 2010 the post-World War II baby boom will be reaching retirement age (Ball, 1975).

The changing demographic structure of the United States population has significant implications on the cost of the Social Security program itself. Projections from the Social Security Administration estimate that the combined employer-employee cost for the Old Age Survivors and Disability Insurance (OASDI) program alone will be 28.6 percent of taxable payrolls by the year 2050. This is a substantial increase from 1976, when the cost of the OASDI program represented only 10.6 percent of earning taxed by Social Security (Munnell, 1978). Half of these expected cost increases can be attributed to the shifting demographic structure of the population (Munnel, 1978). Essentially, the cost burden on the working population is aggravated because fewer people are and will be called upon to pay the increasing expenditures of Social Sec. urity.

The age structure and its implications are immutable. Early retirement or the age of retirement, however, are factors which are subject to manipulation. In light of this, as early as 1975, the Advisory Council on Social Security considered the possibility of a phase-in program for raising the age of full benefit entitlement from 65 to 68 by 2023. A move in the direction of involuntary delayed retirement was considered a viable means to: 1) reduce the combined Social Security tax rate, 2) reduce the burden on future taxpayers, and 3) improve the economic welfare of elderly by shortening the period over which they would normally receive reduced retirement income (Herzog, 1978; Munnell,

1978).

The proposal for rasing the normal retirement age has won support from key administrators, policy strategists, and economists, including former Social Security Administration Director, Robert Ball, former Treasury Secretary, William E. Simon (Gelb, 1977), Robert Clark (Donnelly, 1979), and the National Commission on Social Security (SCACA, 1980). While the suggested phasing-in process and the suggested age increase may vary with different proposals, the general notion is firmly established as a necessary revision to ameliorate the fiscal burden of the retiring post-World War II baby generation by 2010 to 2020.

In December of 1979 the Advisory Council on Social Security returned once again to suggestions for raising the normal age of retirement under Social Security. The Council's final wording of their proposal was:

> A narrow majority of the council urges that serious consideration be given to enactment now of an increase in the normal retirement age under Social Security that would become effective at about the turn of the century (SCA(A), 1980).

The council proposed the following strategy for this phased increase: beginning in the year 2000, the retirement age will be increased by two months each year until 2018 when the normal retirement age would be 68. Under this plan the council recommended the continuation of the delayed retirement credit for persons retiring after age 65, but proposed actuarial reduction in benefits for people retiring before 68. This would cause the benefits of a person who continued working until age 68 in 2018 to be the same as those of a person retiring today, but people who retire before age 68 would receive benefits lower than those of people who retire between 65 and 69 under present law (SCA(A), 1980). As you can see this issue is complex and the proposal itself, equally complex.

The arguments most frequently cited in favor of the Social Security Council's recommendations are varied and include the following:

1. People are living longer today than they were when the Social Security program was created and age 65 was chosen as the normal eligibility age.

   Today, as a result of medical advances, a higher standard of living, less physically demanding work, and a shorter workweek, the life span of Americans has been lengthened. In 1900 the average life expectancy at birth was 47 years. In contrast, for persons born in 1976 the average life expectancy was 72 (Rhine, 1978:22). Life expectancy varies for men and women. Based on death rates in 1976 the average life expectancy at birth was 69 years for males and almost 77 years for females. As a result of an overall lengthening of life span, increasingly large proportions of the population are living for seven and eight or more decades.

2. Raising the normal retirement age under Social Security will relieve the unbearable demands which the "baby-boom" generation will undoubtedly place on the Social Security program. This strain on the system is expected as a result of the diminishing number of workers available to support the expanding number of retired people. In this case a phased increase in the normal retirement age is considered preferable to tax increases or benefit cuts. Specifically, raising the retirement age to 68 would reduce estimated costs of Social Security from 16.24 percent of payroll to 14.5 percent by 2030 (SCA(B), 1980).

3. If radical changes are necessary to "save" Social Security then they should be made far in advance of their implementation so that tax payer's plans and expectations will not be disrupted. A gradual program for raising the retirement age, starting in the year 2000, is felt to be a fair proposal. Most supporters agree that the change should be enacted now, but not be made effective until the distant future, when the need for reform will be greatest. This philosophy permits a sufficient period of time for people to be aware of the planned changes and to prepare for them.

Arguments against proposals to raise the normal retirement age illustrate a distinct disadvantage for minorities should recommendations for a phased age increase be accepted and enacted. The arguments include the following:

1. Raising the eligibility age for full benefits ignores the fact that many people are forced to retire early because of disability or because they can't find jobs. Social Security data indicates that a significant porportion of workers claiming early retirement benefits do so because of poor health. · In addition, almost one-fifth of all men who claim early retirement benefits at age 62 have been out of work for 12 months or more. Compounding these problems is the fact that a great many early retirees have histories of low earnings.

2. Raising the eligibility age for full benefits is actually a benefit cutback which will fall most heavily on today's workers who are paying higher taxes for those benefits, and who expect to be able to retire at age 65 or before. Essentially this argument points to the fact that raising the normal retirement age will affect the very people, those under age 40, who are now being asked to pay larger Social Security taxes over their working lifetimes. This is certainly no way to build confidence in the Social Security System.

3. Forcing people to delay retirement to age 68 is an unnecessarily coercive way of keeping older workers on the job. Those not in favor of a mandatory increased eligibility age urge that there are better ways to encourage older workers to continue on the job. Opponents to the reform suggest that by the turn of the century

employers will make work more attractive to older persons because the size of the traditional working age population will have dim-insished. Finally, to penalize those who can't work until age 65, let alone some higher age, would constitute a deprivation to those unable to respond to an unswerving inducement.

What are the implications for minority groups should the eligibility age be raised? Very simply, the burden of raising the normal age of retirement under' Social Security would fall most heavily on minorities. Compared to all other groups, the minority elderly can be characterized as unable to work until age 68!

Older minority group workers experience special labor force problems, including: generally higher levels of unemployment; more frequent labor force withdrawal; more involuntary part-time employment; more frequent health problems; and finally, "double jeopardy" encounters with combined ageism and racism (U.S. Department of Labor, 1979).

Labor force problems, such as these, are only accentuated by the fact that older minority group workers tend to have more dependence than their Anglo counterparts. Although the relative poor health of minority group members, as well as patterns of extended periods unemployment and part-time work compel these populations to accept early retirement benefits under Social Security, these conditions are sometimes offset by their greater economic need to remain in the labor force—as a result of higher proportions of dependents.

While proponents for the acceptance of reforms to raise the eligibility age suggest that improved life expectancy rates logically support such a move, data from the National Center for Health Statistics (NCHS) demonstrate that concommitant health status has not improved. Indeed, people may be living longer, but with increased incidence of acute conditions and chronic illness (Hsaio, 1980). In addition, disability days and restricted activity days for people age 65 and over have remained unchanged over the last ten years (Hsaio, 1980).

Policymakers and researchers alike have erroneously equated the increase in life expectancy with improvements in health status. Nowhere is this misinterpretation more severe than in characterization of minority groups. Among blacks death rates continue to be much higher than for whites. In addition, the 1975 figure from the NCHS showed that life expectancy at birth for black males was only 60 years. This was 7.9 years less than for white males (SCA(B), 1980).

Large numbers of minority group workers are employed in hazardous jobs, requiring strenuous physical labor. These jobs take a heavy toll on the health of minority older workers, leading to forced involuntary early retirement. In testimony before the House Ways and Means Subcommittee on Oversight, Professor Hsaio put it very eloquently:

> Too frequently those who advocate later retirement policy are armchair theorists. Their jobs require the physical exertion of sitting at a desk, lifting a 3-ounce pencil, in a modern air-conditioned office. The mental exertion consists of reading and writing memorandums and conducting discourse through a telephone line. They have never experienced the exhaustion of lifting 50 lb. boxes for eight hours a day, or continuously operating a pneu-

matic press. Yet they assume 65-year-old workers can continue to lift those weights or operate a heavy machine until age 68 (Hsaio, 1980).

Professor Hsaio suggests that two groups of older workers would suffer most should the normal retirement age be increased. One group is the people whose health has deteriorated but who are not yet eligible for disability benefits. Another group is the workers whose jobs require strenuous physical efforts, most of them in blue collar jobs. Need I point out that Professor Hsaio has just described the majority of older minority group workers.

Members of minority groups are under-represented in certain Social Security Programs—particularly the retirement program. For example, Social Security Administration figures provided to the National Center on the Black Aged show that blacks represent only 10.3 percent of all beneficiaries though they constitute 11.6 percent of the overall United States population (SCA(B), 1980). Among persons receiving retirement benefits, blacks account for only 7.8 percent. Low participation in the retirement program is generally attributable to the fact that blacks (and most other minority groups) tended to work at jobs not covered by Social Security until very recently and that the mortality rate before the age of current eligibility for early or normal retirement benefits is very high among blacks. At the same time, the effects of hazardous work performed by minorities and the higher morbidity rates account for the fact that blacks represent 16.5 percent of disabled workers and dependents, 20.8 percent of the children of retired and deceased workers, and 20.1 percent of the widowed mothers and fathers of young children receiving benefits (SCA(B), 1980). Raising the age for full eligibility of Social Security benefits would only exacerbate these conditions.

Members of the Advisory Council themselves have proposed that the impact on minority groups of changes in the Social Security program should receive explicit attention. At the same time, however, the December 1979 report from the council stated that the council had examined allegations that minorities fare less well under Social Security and concluded that this assertion was unfounded (Reports of the 1979 Advisory Council on Social Security: 1980). Under these circumstances it is difficult to tell exactly where the council stands on minority issues. The council was willing to report that a shorter life expectancy among minorities means that they are "somewhat less likely" than others to receive Social Security benefits. However, the Council pointed out that this is offset by the fact that minority workers are more likely to receive disability and survivor's benefits. For persons devoting their lifetime of labor to strenuous and hazardous work, is it fair that their inability to receive normal retirement benefits, due to their shortened life expectancy, be offset by disability payments?

The Social Security benefit formula has been structured so that it provides workers with lower earnings and a higher benefit relative to their previous earnings. Thus, as long as minorities continue to be paid less or to experience more unemployment than the average worker, the weighting in the benefit formula provides minorities the advantage of higher benefits relative to taxes paid. What the council conveniently fails to point out is that even with benefit formulas which work to the favor of persons with low incomes, when the basic income is so low that even with a weighted formula built in, the amount of benefits minorities receive from Social Security is still less—with blacks receiving 70 percent of the benefits of whites (SCA (B), 1980).

To offset the potentially adverse consequences of an increased eligibility age the Advisory Council on Social Security has recommended the following:

1. Liberalize the definition of disability; in particular develop a definition of disability for the SSI program that is less strict than the definition under Title II;

2. Bring SSI benefits up to the poverty line; and,

3. Provide for long term unemployment compensation, starting at age 60 or 55 and paid until 65 or 68.

It is significant to note that the Social Security Disability program has been identified as a target for cuts under the Reagan Administration. Reagan proposes tightening eligibility for disability benefits and limiting benefit amounts. The chances of this budget cut being accepted are good (*Time*, March 2, 1981). Who will be the victims of these proposals if enacted? Undoubtedly, they will be older members of minority groups. This proposal would put many older minority workers into a king of "never-never land"—forced out of employment due to poor health and disabilities, not eligible for even early retirement benefits (at current standards), and not eligible for disability payments under Social Security. With the enactment of legislation to raise the normal retirement age seemingly eminent, an understanding of the negative consequences for minorities of modification of the disability program is critically needed from the Reagan Administration.

Alternative strategies for preserving the financial soundness of the Social Security program have been suggested and include:

1. To index Social Security benefits by using the Consumer Price Index instead of wages under the present law (Hsaio, 1980);

2. To eliminate early retirement benefits altogether by raising the age for early retirement by one month each year for 36 years so that by 2015 there would be no early retirement benefits allowable;

3. To liberalize or eliminate the earnings test;

4. To tax Social Security benefits in the same way private pensions are taxed; and

5. To extend coverage to all new federal, state and local and non-profit organization employees.

Each of these proposals in some way would perpetuate the already disadvantaged status of minority older workers under Social Security.

Planners of retirement policy often use a metaphor to describe the optimum retirement situation. They describe this optimum condition as a three-legged stool, with Social Security as the first leg, pensions as the second leg and savings as the third leg. For older minority persons the first leg is already short and with very few minorities drawing private pension benefits, the second and third legs are usually missing.

No one would argue with the statement that the Social Security system is facing long-term deficits. By 2050 the expected value of the tax revenues will fall short by a trillion dollars and if nothing is done now, this funding deficit will require doubling payroll taxes early in next century. To offset this crisis a shortening of the retirement period, through enactment of a phases increase in the normal retirement age, is viewed as a viable alternative. For each year the retirement period is shortened $250-$300 billion of the deficit will be saved (Boskin, 1980). But what will be the deficit in terms of human suffering for members of minority groups if this proposal is hurriedly accepted? We must be careful not to leave the policy-making to such policymakers as Mr. Aaron, President of the Advisory Council on Social Security, who has said that:

> Social Security cannot be expected to assure an above-poverty level income to workers who do not spend most of their working lifetimes under the system, under the Social Security System, or who work only part time during most of their careers.

The development and evaluation of alternate strategies is critical before any implementation of an involuntary delayed retirement program. Creative alternatives have been developed and implemented in other nations. One of the oldest flexible retirement provisions has been the payment of benefits before the normal retirement age to workers in arduous or hazardous occupations.

In France, for example, legislation enabled manual workers with 42 years of employment, with 5-15 years before retirement performed in strenuous labor, to retire at age 60 and receive a pension equal to that usually payable at age 65 (SCA (B) 1980). With clear drawbacks to ethnic-specific legislation, this type of legislation, which differentiates by occupation characteristics, may be preferable. I have described the situation in France only as an example; we must now discover our own solutions. The upcoming 1981 White House Conference on Aging provides one forum in which to do just that, and I urge that the issue be addressed.

References

Ball, R.M. Social security financing, *Public Welfare*, 1975, *33 (4)*, 10-15.

Boskin, M. The long-run social security financing problem and retirement behavior: Summary. Testimony presented to Subcommittee on Oversight, U.S. House of Representatives, September 10, 1980.

Brotman, H.B. Every ninth American. Developments in aging: 1978. A report of the Special Committee on Aging, United States Senate, Washington, D.C.: U.S. Government Printing Office, 1979.

Campbell, R.R. *Social security promise and reality.* Stanford, CA, Hoover, Institution Press, 1977.

Clark, R.L., & Spengler, J. Economic responses to population aging with special emphasis on retirement policy. In R.L. Clark (ED.) *Retirement policy in an aging society*, Durham, North Carolina: Duke University Press, 1980.

Donnelly, H.H. The graying of America: Aging U.S. population poses threat to retirement systems. *Congressional Quarterly Weekly Report*, March 17, 1979, *37 (11)*, 441-449.

Feldstein, M. Toward a reform of social security. *The Public Interest*, 1975, *40*, 75-95.

Flaim, P.O., & Fullerton, H.N. Labor force projections in 1990: Three possible paths, *Monthly Labor Review*, 1978, *36 (1)*, 25-35.

From the schools to the sewers: the budgeting survey would affect just about everybody. *Time*, March 2, 1981, 16-18.

Gelb, R.D. When compulsory retirement at 65 is ended. *Harvard Business Review*, July-August, 1977, 6-9.

Herzog, B.R. Providing income and opportunities for work: Future policy choices. In B.R. Herzog (Ed.) *Aging and income.* New York: Human Sciences Press, 1978.

Hsiao, William C. Raising the retirement age—Who will bear the burden? Testimony presented to Subcommittee on Oversight, U.S. House of Representatives, September 10, 1980.

Munnell, A.H. *The future of social security.* Washington, D.C.: The Brookings Institution, 1977.

Newsletter of the CASE center for gerontological studies/The Graduate School and University Center. The City University of New York, November-December 1979.

Quinn, J.F. Microeconomic determinants of early retirement, A cross-sectional view of white married men, *The Journal of Human Resources*, 1977, *12*, 329-346.

Reports of the 1979 advisory council on social security. *Social Security Bulletin*, 1980, *43 (2)*, 3-15.

Special Committee on Aging, United States Senate. SCA (A), *Emerging options for work and retirement policy.* Washington, D.C.: U.S. Government Printing Office, 1980.

Special Committee on Aging, United States Senate. SCA(B). Oversight on Recommendations of 1979 Social Security Advisory Council. Washington, D.C.: U.S. Government Printing Office, 1980.

Sheppard, H.L., & Rix, S.E. *The graying of working america.* New York: The Free Press, 1977.

Singer, J.W. A brighter future for older workers, *National Journal*, 1978, *10*, 1722-1725.

Spengler, J.J. Stationary population and changes in age structure: Implications for the economic security of the aged. Paper prepared for the National Science Foundation, 1975.

U.S. Department of Labor. *Employment related problems of older workers: A research strategy.* R & D Monograph 73. Employment and Training Division, Washington, D.C.: U.S. Government Printing Office, 1979.

V
Conclusions

INTRODUCTION

This chapter is composed of the individual Work Session Recommendations, the Action Session Summaries, and the Final Resolutions. The Session Recommendations were developed by those individuals who participated in the specific workshop. These recommendations were not formally shared with, nor sanctioned by, the total conference body. However, the original Work Session Recommendations were later consolidated into Action Session Summaries which were presented to all of the participants during a general session. As a result of these efforts, the Conference Resolutions were developed, refined and ratified by the participants during the final general session of the meeting.

WORK SESSIONS RECOMMENDATIONS

I. ACCESS AND UTILIZATION OF SOCIAL SERVICES

Workshop Presentors:
Valerie L. Levy
Jessie McClure
Rudy Arrieta

1. Identify and assign a minority elderly individual to be a member on all workshop panels during future IMA conferences to represent their needs and concerns.

2. Develop a practice forum for minority elderly and service providers to discuss successful techniques and strategies for reaching and serving minority elderly.

3. Change the language in the Older Americans Act that requires participation of elderly on advisory boards so that *decision-making power* is given to minority elderly.

4. Mandate that federally assisted programs provide accurate information on their compliance to laws and legislation and where non-compliance is observed federal monies should be removed and legal action taken.

II. MULTI-PURPOSE SENIOR CENTERS

Workshop Presentors:
Bill Chin
Evalyn Greb

1. Ensure that a fair share of funds for multi-purpose senior centers and focal points be designated for the low income and/or minority communities.

2. Ensure that employment opportunities be available for residents served by the Center.

3. Need for clear explanation of the Older Americans Act and other legislation affecting the older citizens, e.g. state units on aging making this available.

III. NUTRITION WORKSHOP

Workshop Facilitators:
Lucious McCalpine
Barry Donenfeld
Esperanza Eugenio

Recommendations
1.   Eligibility criteria should be enacted for Nutrition Services.

   a.   SSI should be the basic criteria for membership donations.

   b.   Those who do not qualify for SSI should be requested to pay a fee set by the local project council.

2.   Greater Access to Nutrition Services

   a.   Nutrition Sites should be located where the need is greatest.

   b.   Census Tracts Surveys should be used in determining where sites should be located.

   c.   To facilitate access to nutrition services in high crime areas, part of the C_1 and C_2 budgets should allow for security services, outreach and transportation.

3.   Reenactment of the pre-1978 Amendment language regarding "Minority" back into the OAA emphasizing provision of Minority Services in proportion to minority population.

4.   Transportation for Nutrition Programs should be placed back into C_1 budget.

5.   Strengthen nutrition education functions of the Nutrition Programs with some basic guidelines (more specific) from Health and Human Services.

6.   Project Councils should be made up of ethnic minorities in relation to their proportions to the general populace in the Planning and Service Areas.

IV. HOUSING

Workshop Presentors:
Charles Martinez
Rachel Wong
Lupe Bickley

Problem Identification

The existing policy governing issues related to the rights of elderly to access of housing resources is not well defined and subject to inconsistent and arbitrary decision outcomes at the local, state and federal levels. In addition, there does not exist any machinery of accountability which elderly can use to challenge the decision-making bureaucrats and politicians who are implementing the existing policy.

Proposed Goal

To ensure that elderly fully understand their rights (1) regarding access to housing resources as well as (2) status as elderly persons to live in comfortable and affordable housing. In addition, a greater number of legal and political resources which will ensure accountability of decision makers is needed.

1.   Action Steps: Local Level

Local housing commissioners must be required to actively *solicit* and receive input from elderly constituency groups on decisions pertaining to housing issues. These "input facilitation" activities must be stringently monitored to ensure participation. Failure to solicit input should be a condition to negate any decision made by the local policy making body (i.e., Housing Commission).

2.   Action Steps: State Level

State senators and assemplyment must take a more active role in making sure elderly are informed of the pressing housing issues at hand. A mechanism must be developed by citizen interest groups to ensure elderly are well informed of the voting record of their state representatives on issues affecting their housing needs. Notification of public hearings must be done in a fashion which is in line with governmental regulations. These public hearing notifications must be done in a manner which will ensure direct contact with the elderly segment of the state.

3.   Action Steps: Federal Level

Similar actions instituted at the state and local levels to ensure accountability of federal bureaucrats and politicians must be addressed. Summaries of voting records and stands on housing issues must be made available to elderly citizen interest groups (or dissemination, analysis, and discussion. Consideration should be also made to providing federal economic incentives to legal professionals who make a significant time commitment to advocating for the housing rights and needs of elderly, particularly minority elderly.

In all instances, it must be emphasized that active participation and coalition building of elderly citizens as well as advocates for the elderly is also required.

V.   LONG-TERM CARE

Workshop Presentors:
Jennie Chin Hansen
Vladimir Einisman
Azelia French-Upshaw

1.   Call AoA to account to the legislature mandate which is to determine needs and establish services which will address the issues encountered by minority and other truly needy elderly.

2.   That people who are in actual need of services receive them as contrasted to supporting those who happen to be more aggressive in using available services.

3.   That active participation and coalition building by elderly minority citizens as well as advocates for the elderly be implemented in communities.

4.   That mechanisms that have been already established to ensure accountability to minority elderly be empowered to implement their responsibility and assure that consequences will occur as a result of any infractions found.

5.   That fragmentation of service delivery systems be corrected in order to provide a case management system that directly evolves from the service need of the minority elder rather than what resources happen to be available in the area.

VI. EMPLOYMENT

Workshop Presentors:
Sharon Moriwaki
Sandra Nathan

Employment
1. Expand OAA Title V to include more funding as well as change regulations to include private sector placements (which will increase unsubsidized placements) as well as substantial training/retraining of participants.

2. Assess needs of minority elders, particularly the non-English or limited English speaking re: employment needs, interests, skills, and provide funding under Title V to provide more funding to states to develop jobs for these groups.

Strategies
1. Advocacy ethnic organizations must train minority elders at the local community levels to understand and impact all levels of government.

2. Provide tax incentives to employers for training/retraining, retaining and hiring minority elderly.

Recommendations Relative to Volunteerism
Older minorities are increasing in number and represent a significant untapped resource. If they are to be encouraged to continue productive involvement on a volunter basis, the following recommendations are suggested:

1. Increase Budget appropriations for ACTIONS Older Americans Volunteer Programs (Foster Grandparents, Senior Companions and Retired Senior Volunteers).

2. Change age requirements for eligibility in ACTION'S three programs from 60 to 55.

3. Increase the stipend level for volunteers as the cost of volunteering increases (periodic i.e. annual review).

4. Encourage Community Service and Voluntary organizations to establish career ladders so volunteers can move from volunteer to part-time or full-time employment.

VII. LEGAL SERVICES

Workshop Presentor:
Wilford Wilson

Recommendations for Policy Change: Older Americans Act

1. Funds should be appropriated and designated in order to assure the provision of *affordable* legal services to elderly persons.

    a. State and local area agencies on aging should be mandated to increase appropriations for legal services.

    b. Appropriations should include monies targeted for outreach programs which would link seniors to available legal services.

2. National, state and local entities should coordinate with bar associations to ensure participation of private and public attorneys in rendering affordable legal services to elderly persons.

3. Education and training should be provided to attorneys, paralegals, and to the elderly individuals regarding the entire spectrum of legal entitlements available to the elderly population.

VIII. TRAINING

Workshop Presentors:
E. Percil Stanford
Frances Kobata
David Pritchard

1. Provide appropriate training and education regarding minorities for professionals and paraprofessionals working with OAA programs, as well as others providing services to the elderly, and the elderly themselves.

2. Insure accessibility to educational and training programs for minority elderly and/or those working in their behalf. This should be visible in all OAA titled programs.

3. The educational network (formal and informal) should encompass culturally diverse subject matter regarding minority elderly in the areas of research, materials development and programming.

4. Training monies should be tied to each section of the OAA.

IX. RESEARCH

Workshop Presentors:
Jean Crawford
José Cuellar
Maurice Jackson
John Red Horse
Antonio Rey
Sylvia Schwitters

1. The priority research question should be: how do we increase and organize the fiscal resources (money to older people) to develop a minority aging perspective that ensures the strength of elders will build minority communities.

2. The priority research area should be systems analysis of the fiscal and monetary policies of the federal government to identify gaps in established policies to set fiscal priorities and to conduct ongoing analysis to monitor responses and track policy.

X. NATURAL SUPPORT SYSTEMS

Workshop Presentors:
Wesley Ishikawa
Esther Langston
Ramon Salcido

Recommendations

1. Do not accept cutbacks in aging programs for 1981 but press for an increase in funding levels for aging programs, as funding levels for aging programs were/are indadequate for the current aging populations, and the aging population is increasing in numbers.

2. There should be more research and training on natural networks for their utilization with formal service systems. Incorporate natural support networks into prevailing service systems in local communities. Resources such as tax incentives, stipends, etc. should be developed for identifying and strengthening these systems.

XI. THE SOCIO-ECONOMIC STATUS OF THE MINORITY ELDERLY: STRATEGIES TO DETERMINE BUDGETARY NEEDS

Workshop Presentors:
Duran Bell
Lodis Rhodes

1. A solid economic base for elders is needed rather than base subsistence provisions in Social Security. The prospect may be for increasing longevity by reducing stresses attendant to poverty. It may also reduce the extent of overutilization of natural support networks, thus providing more choice.

2. That a tax credit be considered for families caring for older persons in their own home as an incentive to present premature institutionalization.

3. Consider expansion of the tax deduction for support of elderly other than blood relatives.

4. That minority elderly not be penalized by Social Security for monies earned in addition to their S.S. benefit.

5. Tax laws be rewritten not to penalize elders for receiving money from family members and that tax credits (exemption or other write-offs) be allowed to those who support older family memebers. The write-offs would be limited to a reasonable living rate of $10,000 and dollar for dollar for health cost payments.

XII. INCREASING THE NATIONAL AGE OF RETIREMENT

Workshop Presentors:
Martha McFadden
Fernando Torres-Gil

1. Mandatory Social Security coverage for all federal, state and local employees.

2. Development and implementation of a mandatory national pension program.

3. Do not raise the age of eligibility for full benefits under the Social Security system until programs are *in place* which will offset the expected negative consequences for minorities should this proposal be accepted.

3a. Differential retirement aged based on occupation.

4. That the National Minority organizations accept these recommendations and advocate in their behalf through the channels available to them.

ACCESS AND UTILIZATION OF SOCIAL SERVICES, MULTI-PURPOSE SENIOR CENTERS, LEGAL SERVICES

Esther Jones Langston, Ph.D.

1. Participation of minority seniors at the IMA—revise format to hear from minority seniors on panels.

2. I.M.A. along with other groups should provide training sessions to help seniors participate in a variety of ways in programs designed for them. Training in advocacy.

3. Change language in OAA to provide for decision-making process mandate for seniors as consumers.

    a. Learn techniques for influencing political change and how to communicate with politicians at all levels.

    b. Educate participants re: broad potential of advisory councils, i.e., demand clarification.

    c. Use senior centers operations and manual of NCOA for training purposes.

    d. Study and analyze the OAA of the State to understand the potential of advocacy.

4. Compliance Problems:

    a. Develop strategies for monitoring activities of organizations to get facts (do your homework).

    b. Formulate complaints in a way that will impact on the release of funds.

    c. Get legal advice.

    d. Learn specifics of funding sources.

5. The human service model will address the needs of the elderly. An age stratified service delivery model has the greatest impact on minority aged who are in the greatest need.

LONG-TERM CARE, HOUSING AND NUTRITION

Jennie Chin Hansen, M.S.

1. Call AoA to account to the legislative mandate which is to determine needs and establish services which will address the issues encountered by minority and other truly needy elderly.

2. That people who are in actual need of services receive them as contrasted to supporting those who happen to be more aggressive in using available services.

3. That active participation and coalition building by elderly minority citizens as well as advocates for the elderly be implemented in communities.

4. That mechanisms that have been already established to ensure accountability to minority elderly be empowered to implement their responsibility and assure that consequences will occur as a result of any infractions found.

5. That fragmentation of service delivery systems be corrected in order to provide a case management system that directly evolves from the service need of the minority elder rather than what resources happen to be available in the area.

EMPLOYMENT, TRAINING AND RESEARCH

John Red Horse, Ph.D.

1. Develop appropriate education and training for seniors and those who are working with them.

2. Insure access by minority elders into training programs. Train minority people so indigenous communities can help themselves.

3. Develop a curriculum that is relevant to culturally diverse elders.

4. There is a need to increase funding for employment of bilingual elders.

5. Develop tax incentives for employees to hire elders.

6. Develop a career ladder in voluntary work. Develop a new definition of volunteerism.

7. Do research to determine how much money is being saved by natural support systems. Develop a dollar value on this system.

INCREASING THE NATIONAL AGE OF RETIREMENT; ECONOMIC STATUS; AND NATURAL SUPPORTS

Fred Anderson, DSW

1. That the eligibility age for retirement not be raised to 68 for benefits under Social Security and that recognition of the impact of hazardous occupations such as construction be factored into the age equation. A different retirement age, based on occupation, should be considered given that disability funds are now being paid to individuals in certain hazardous occupations.

2. That a tax credit be considered for families now carring for older persons in their own home as an incentive to prevent premature institutionalization or home care services.

3. That all persons including members of Congress participate in a national private pension program in addition to Social Security which is equitable and uniform and/or amend private pension programs to prevent pension fraud on the part of employees and unions.

4. That minority elderly not be penalized by Social Security earned in addition to their Social Security retirement benefits.

5. That natural support systems development include the community leadership in the development and implementation of service delivery plans and their research funds.

6. Natural support systems should not substitute for the overwhelming need for financial security and integrity for the minority elderly.

7. Provide broad research discretion to identify natural support networks in each minority community and to develop plans for their interaction with current service delivery systems.

FINAL RESOLUTIONS

We, the participants at the Eighth National Institute on Minority Aging, are dedicated to ensuring equivalent distribution of available resources to that segment of the older population in greatest social and economic need. Although there has been the emergence of a group identified as minorities from European countries (Euro-ethnics), elder minorities are by definition a composite of such groups as American Indians, black Americans, Hispanics, and Pacific/Asians. It is necessary to delineate the significant differences in the experiences of people of color who have systematically, through legislation, policy decisions, and executive fiat, been excluded from meaningful participation in society throughout their lives. The ethnic minority elders therefore require that society at large address their needs as a priority.

We therefore strongly recommend that:

1. Older minorities, the majority of whom have disproportionate needs, be recognized and considered as the truly needy.

2. Older minorities, the preponderance of whom are poor, must receive services that are based on their cultural and philosophical heritages and their legal rights.

3. Older minorities and those working in their behalf must be represented in parity on the 1981 White House Conferance on Aging national and regional advisory boards, technical committees, and in the significant policy-making presentations.

The above resolutions are forwarded from the conference participants for your information and reaction. The participants would like to receive a response regarding your position on the above statements. More specifically, will you support policies and decisions which acknowledge the fact that elder minorities are represented disproportionately in the lower socio-economic strata, and are also in need? Further, are you willing to support the continuation of the older minorities' significant involvement on advisory committees and boards at all levels of government?

The Participants at the
Eighth National Institute on Minority Aging